A Wanderful Life

Your Guide to RV Living

Barbara Wentzell Jaquith

Cover photo credit
Debbie and Paul Murray

Advisory assistance:

Livingston, Texas

ISBN: 978-0-9961520-8-2

Author's Note

I've relied upon my memory to the best of my ability, notes, and some audio-taped interviews from our traveling time to compose this book. However, I've changed the names of some places, and the names and identifying details of some individuals to protect their privacy.

Table of Contents

Introduction: Sharing the Fire   1

Chapter One: Percolation   7

Chapter Two: What is Mobile Community?   15

Chapter Three: Is the Wandering Lifestyle Right for You?   29

Chapter Four: Family Matters   43

Chapter Five: The Weight of Attachments   53

Chapter Six: Rehearsal Dinner   65

Chapter Seven: Wandering Mindfully   77

Chapter Eight: Choice or Necessity?   89

Chapter Nine: Creating and Sustaining Mobile Community   101

Chapter Ten: Chance Encounters   115

Chapter Eleven: The Wanderlust   129

Chapter Twelve: One of Those Days   141

Chapter Thirteen: The Right Fit   151

Chapter Fourteen: Two by Two; Pets Aboard   165

Chapter Fifteen: Where the Road Ends   175

Dedication   187

Acknowledgments   189

About the Author   191

Introduction: Sharing the Fire

Once all the power goes out, there will still be human beings standing together around a campfire, playing acoustic guitars.
- Jim James

There was never any question that I would someday belong to a community of nomads. Many of my most treasured memories have been made sitting around a campfire with friends and family. All it takes is a newly lit fire to spark the recollection of conversations at fire circles from decades past. There are cherished memories of our small children toasting marshmallows on sticks, laughing irreverently with friends over a glass of wine after those children were snug in bed in tents. Other times, I was sitting solo by the fire, trying to figure out where life should go next.

In meditation, I only need to breathe deeply and imagine a crackling campfire to re-live tender times when friends gathered after dark to talk and sing and laugh around the magic of fire. Hearing the snap of burning logs again, I recall the smoke of past campfires rising and descending as it settles its pine essence deep into thick wool sweaters. The fire embraces all who come to the circle in a group hug. It turns its attention first to the east and then shifts to the west in answer to the direction given by the breeze. However, the fire always keeps its smoky arm around the whole shared circle.

A long-ago guitar plays the songs of my youth and once again, the passion of the debates we engaged in is real. I savor the compassion we showed one another in times of sadness or need and the joy with which we celebrated personal triumphs and accomplishments. Even the thought of a campfire has the power to lull me into a meditative state where the poignant past is just a sigh away and old friends gather around the fire.

There is a special place along the Maine coast where my heart healed and my life found direction in the company of friends who camped together for seven summers. The kids had grown up; I was newly divorced, single for the first time in my adult life and ready to have some fun. Our group of campers gathered around the fire at the end of the workweek every Friday and Saturday night. On Fridays, we decompressed and put our week-days into perspective so that we could get about the business of enjoying the weekend. On Saturdays, we ate pot luck after long beach days and then settled in for a campfire that went well into the night. These were rowdy times full of laughter and pranks that more than once elicited a stern warning from the camp-ground owner to quiet down or else. Two of those friends, first met around an Ogunquit campfire, are my dearest and closest friends to this day. When we get together and reminisce now, the conversation inevitably turns to those nostalgic times. Like all of life's seasons, those Maine summer campfires were unique in their own time and place.

But before Maine, there was another treasured time of fires and friendship. There is a point of singularity for every adolescent when we awaken to see a first glimpse of what will be our life's passion. I discovered what would be mine that summer with Tommy.

Tommy was my brother's friend before he became my friend. He used to hang around our house when we were teenagers. He and my brother Bill would go joyriding in Dad's old white Impala. But I never noticed him until one day we discovered our common interests. Tommy loved to draw and so did I. The day that he showed up with an art pad and charcoal pencils, I saw him in a wholly different light. We both wanted to go to art

2

school and I know he would have done so if not for the draft. He also loved a big roaring campfire. Soon, my brother's friend became my pal too.

We grew up dead center in the heart of New Hampshire, just a few miles from a secluded state park in the White Mountain National Forest. The rules were lax and weekend supervision by the Forest Service back then was non-existent. We lived in a small town in rural New Hampshire and there wasn't much for teens to do on a Saturday night. As a result, we often congregated out at the park around a campfire. It was just a small group of nature-loving kids who felt most at home outdoors. We were generally law-abiding and not excessively unruly. Still, it's puzzling that no one ever questioned what we might be doing out in the woods lighting fires.

Our purpose was rather innocent. We were there to sing. Tommy played the guitar and we took turns calling out the songs. Wren accompanied on harmonica. The log seating served as percussion and Brett drummed out a backbeat. A couple of kids had exceptional voices and the rest of us blended in as best we could with more passion than talent. There was plenty of beer and sometimes a bit of weed and whatever food we could confiscate from home to bring for pot luck snacks. We experimented with being activists, scholars, intellectuals, nerds. We were not the cool kids, but we did think that some of us might be the ones to make a difference in the world. Social change was a reoccurring theme in our conversation. It is extraordinary that for most of this group of teens, making a difference would become a reoccurring theme throughout our lives.

In a circle around the night fires, we sang the songs of the late sixties. Joan Baez, Pete Seeger and Peter, Paul and Mary lyrics drifted towards the heavens on glowing red embers. Tommy led us as we sang the poetry of Dylan and he especially loved

Woody Guthrie's *This Land is Your Land*. We knew those songs by heart; they were the architecture of our budding moral compasses. The artists were the voices of the war resistance. In our naivety, we sincerely believed that these artists and songs were the change agents that would prevail in calming the chaos and insanity of Vietnam.

In addition to the folk artists, Tommy loved Jefferson Airplane. He strummed the guitar and sang, *Go Ask Alice*, Grace Slick's [1] reference to Lewis Carroll's classic *Alice in Wonderland*. Tommy sat on a log, facing the fire with the flames reflecting off his thick oversize glasses. His hair mopped over his face as he looked down at the guitar and drew out notes. Tommy mesmerized us with his talent, bound us together with his sense of purpose and idealism. He was our gangly fearless leader in song, setting the stage for us to bridge the literature, poetry and songs of childhood with the very grown-up topics of sixties culture.

We sat up so close to the heat of those fires that our faces turned red and the knees of our jeans burned hot. In the chilly New Hampshire nights, we talked of the war, of peace and conscientious resistance. We were figuring out our place in the world. Talking it through, we fleshed out hopes and dreams and explored social causes. It wasn't light talk around those fires. These weren't easy times and thus, we weren't light-weight kids. Those campfires forged us into idealistic young adults, bound by the majestic nature surrounding us and the malevolent nature of the times.

The time around the fire from those closing days of childhood in New Hampshire fused kindred teenage souls into kinship based on deep and abiding friendships. Joined at the fire circle, we practiced debating hot topics with respect. We experienced first-hand the healing value of music and voices raised together in song. Harmonizing to Amazing Grace, we grew together into our separate identities. Out of that circle would emerge a Marine, an artist, a healer, a professor, a social worker, an animal rights activist, a committed foster dad/adoptive parent, a comedian, a national park ranger and one tormented alcoholic singer-songwriter, all of whom had been forged by the fire of adolescent angst.

As the seasons passed, we all reached the other side of the bridge to young adulthood. We took different forks in the road and began to follow the individual paths that called to us. We kept in touch as best we could with no cell phones, no Facebook, or any social media of any type. We still somehow managed to loosely keep up with what was happening in each other's lives. When we were all in town at the same time, usually around holidays, we tried to get together, but things weren't ever the same. There were kids and bills and jobs now.

The call came on a frigid Christmas morning when my brother and I had gathered for dinner with our families at my parents' home. It was a short call. When brother Bill hung up, he stared blankly out the picture window in the dining room, looking down on Dad's sleeping garden encased in a crust of icy winter snow. After a moment, he turned and told me that Tommy's father had just called to let us know that Tommy was gone. He was killed while stationed in Thailand on his way to Vietnam. The last ember of that season of life had been snuffed out and there wouldn't be another campfire with our friend. There was no more Alice to ask.

Tommy has been seated beside me at every campfire since that day. The essence of a dear and formative friendship still radiates warm in my heart. We practiced kinship as kids and the truths we discovered remain with me today. I would carry those truths forward and make community the central theme of my life's work. That work began with a group of idealistic hippie kids who knew what it was to strike a match and light the shared fire in the forest of New Hampshire.

Camping with friends has stayed with me as a lifetime passion. My husband Arnie and I are high school buddies who reconnected after 35 years, rekindled our friendship, fell in love and got married. We started camping together right away and began planning for a time after retirement when we could make it a full-time lifestyle. We eased into it for a few years, taking shorter trips and wrestling with the intricate details of a significant life transition. In 2015 we retired, sold our house, put a few things in storage and launched the dream as we set out with our pet family of two dogs, Hana and Wicca and a crazy African Grey parrot named Cracker to call an RV our home.

Since then, our mutual love of being in nature has brought us into contact with many new people. We've often struck up casual conversations with fellow travelers only to find that we know some of the same people, or enjoy some of the same places and experiences. We've welcomed folks from all walks of life to our fire. It's a communal experience that's so much a part of the human DNA. By reading this book, you now share our fire. Welcome.

[1] https://www.allmusic.com/artist/grace-slick-mn0000194743/biography

Chapter One
Percolation
Thinking About a Full-Time RV Lifestyle

"Ideas percolate. Through natural selection, the best ones survive."
- Andrew Lo

Baby boomers are entering retirement in droves eager to realize their dreams of travel and exploration. After years of raising kids, paying the mortgage and holding down nine-to-five jobs that many found necessary but uninspiring, they're ready to think about a change. Some embark quite impulsively and never look back, tackling the mobile lifestyle with enthusiasm and confidence, successfully working out the bugs as they go along. Others hit some bumps in the road and realize that the idea could have used some preparation. Like a great cup of coffee, it generally takes a bit of patient percolation to develop this transition smoothly and provide a satisfying experience.

Whether your own decision to adopt an RVing lifestyle is made impulsively or with planning, you undoubtedly are looking forward to experiencing life fully. None of us can know anything about what is yet to come, but we all yearn for happiness. We quest to find that in new vistas and new learning through travel to new inspiring places across this beautiful country. Most people that I interviewed for this book shared that they engaged in a process of sorting through ideas for their travel. They percolated an abundance of ideas and allowed the best to rise to the top naturally over time. I also discovered a common theme that most people wished they had placed more emphasis on planning before they departed.

Perhaps the greatest planning challenge in moving forward in life is letting go of what we'll be leaving behind. It's just reality that we can't pack everything and everyone dear to us into the RV. We must give some thought to what we'll leave behind. It's challenging to focus on what's in the headlights if you're still looking back at what's fading in the tail-lights.

For most of us, moving forward means that we'll be embarking on a grand new adventure, but at the same time, leaving behind much that's familiar. We'll say at least a temporary goodbye to kids and grandkids, good friends of many years, a church family, neighbors, or work colleagues. Familiar places to shop, restaurants and watering holes, social clubs and groups and the family doctor will all change now with your new mobile lifestyle. If connections are essential to you, maybe you're wondering how you'll make the transition and find critical relationships and supports along the road? Where do you even start?

Community isn't happenstance. When you're RVing full time, you'll need to think about it from a whole new perspective. A mobile lifestyle will call you to be purposeful about not only building your community but also about sustaining it. Tolkien's character, Gandalf said, "Not all those who wander are lost." [1] I'd suggest that Tolkien's wanderers were still grounded in a communal group. They had their steadfast traveling companions and connections with those friendly folk they met along the way. Therefore they were never truly lost. It's possible to create a new and dynamic style of community that's just as rich and satisfying as the one you're leaving. We've learned a trick or two for doing just that and we hope to share our insights with you.

It's almost universal to have some reservations about the transition to RVing. But you already have lots of experience with evolutions; this isn't entirely new terrain. You've changed schools, neighborhoods, jobs and relationships. You may have gone from high school to college or work, or you changed jobs, got married, or had kids. You have had to cut ties with what you know and then push through the gap until you settle into what's new. You've done this before and you can do it again- even better this time because you've acquired skills and knowledge along the way.

Planning a transition to RVing is no different. It's a process with a new set of problems and one that demands that you adjust your thinking. Your experience is your most valuable teacher. Percolate on how you handled major changes in the past. Give some thought to what helped you navigate new seasons of life successfully. What made you resilient? What strengths and values can you tap into that will help you thrive amid this next big transition?

Here are some considerations that you might expect to experience as you make the transition to being on the road. These are most helpful when you approach them with an open heart and flexible mindset. Trying to arrange your life exactly as you imagine it seldom works. But the life transitions that you craft with care and self-examination can open you to deeper meaning as you contemplate the nuts and bolts of making this life change.

- Expect to feel some mixed emotions. You'll face a whole new learning curve about the culture of RVing, mechanical aspects of your vehicles, geography you'll cover, etc. In the beginning, it is natural that you will be out of your comfort zone, so don't let that worry or distract you from the excitement of your upcoming adventures.

- Expect to grieve what you're leaving behind, but don't get stuck there. Rather than ruminating about loss, try to focus on where you are now and where you are headed. Yes, some doors will be closing, but close them gently and don't take the time to stare at what's behind them. Consider this time a turning point and get excited about the challenge.

- Expect to feel overwhelmed at times by all that you need to accomplish. Avoid this by taking everything step-by-step. Move on as quickly as possible with the brainstorming and makeover of your new lifestyle.

- Expect to need to acquire some knowledge and support for your decision. Get yourself into active learner mode and start researching all of the information available. Use social media and the first-hand experience of others to absorb expertise from someone who's done this before. YouTube has helpful postings from folks who are already successful wanderers. Learn about their stories and lives and be inspired by their journeys. Join an RVing travel club and begin to collect all of the priceless information from their members and on their websites about the skills and attitudes that may be useful to adopt.

- Expect to need a cheerleader. Gather some allies around you who can support your decision to make this transition. Pick someone who you can trust to give you honest but gentle feedback. Find a trusted listener if you're planning to travel solo. Try to identify a confidant or mentor who takes your life change seriously and can help to make the process less overwhelming.

- Expect some stress. Just because this is a happy transition doesn't mean it comes without any pressure. Even good things can cause stress, so go easy on yourself. Keep up those activities that help you de-stress;

go to the gym, meet friends for coffee, walk the dog, or meditate. This change will be only as stressful as you allow it to be.

- Expect delays and unforeseen circumstances. These happen in every other aspect of life, so they will likely be part of this transition as well. Develop realistic timeframes and reasonable expectations for your shift and then stay purposeful as events unfold. When changes interrupt the flow of your plans, adjust and regroup, keeping your eye on your reward. Different, even better, rewards may result as you adjust to new circumstances. You'll need to be positive, patient and purposeful to make this happen. Savor the act of changing and let that act be your reward.

- Expect to keep the faith. Whatever religious or spiritual path you follow, look to God, your higher power, or your inner wisdom. The terminology doesn't matter. What matters is that you have an inner anchor. Find and keep this place close during your transition so that as you proceed, you learn about your inner self even as you experience more of the outer world through your travels.

During our initial transition to life on the road, Arnie and I decided that defining a purpose for our travels would help us to stay true to our underlying values. It was a time of uncertainty and a compass was needed. After planning and discussing our travel intentions, we decided that our purpose would include four focus areas. We wanted to (1) learn from local history, (2) listen to regional music, (3) savor real food and (4) explore the natural landscape. These topics were the starting point for research about what we wanted to see and where we wanted to go. We've learned through experience that when we devote adequate contemplation to travel decisions, they usually turn out better. With proper planning, we hoped to craft connections that would become our new mobile group of colleagues. That purposefulness has proven to be a good strategy most of the time. Other times, we've chosen to figuratively throw the map out the window and make a sharp right turn down a dirt road to see what's there. Our planning got us to the dirt road and our flexibility got us to the fantastic sunset at the end of it.

Are you a history buff? Do you have a goal of seeing all of the National Parks? Perhaps you would enjoy a visit to all of the presidential libraries or the home stadiums of all of the US baseball teams. Bird watching is a common pastime shared among those who wander. Think about your interests and how you might pursue them further through RVing. You can start to ponder a route that would take you far and wide to the places that would hold meaning for you. Having a goal or purpose will help you keep a forward-focused mindset when the details of making the transition threaten to bog you down.

This books' primary audience may be retiree roadies, but we frequently encounter families who are choosing a mobile life as well. Many parents are homeschooling a generation of kids who are experiencing national parks as their classrooms. We also routinely encounter delightful young professionals, such as traveling nurses or pipeline engineers who are moving from contract job to contract job, seeing the sights along the way.

This book intends to be a guide for all prospective road trekkers who wish to consider the full time wandering lifestyle. The traveling community is diverse and each story is unique. Whoever you are, if you're thinking about traveling in an RV, you'll find helpful advice for planning and executing your transition in the following chapters. Consider it the equivalent of a chat around the campfire where you pick up some useful information to apply to your journey. I hope to offer you some insights from our travels and those of other experienced sojourners we've met along the way. No matter the reason or purpose for your journey, there are some critical questions to ask before you decide that the mobile lifestyle is for you. This book will help you percolate about them.

So who are these people who are living the life you're thinking about adopting? In a recent census survey conducted by the Escapees RV Club [2], respondents offered the following insights into who you'll meet RVing:

> *"As anticipated, most census respondents (57%) identified as being of or more than 65 years of age. When asked how many years they have been RVing, 36% of respondents selected 15+ and 48% of them currently travel full-time. Given these figures, it's reasonable to conclude that many of today's RVers have been on the road at least part-time since their 40s or 50s.*
>
> *Considering how many RVers began traveling in their 40s-50s, it's no surprise that this same age group is on the rise among today's RVing community. Of the 7800 survey respondents, 43% are under 65, the usual age of retirement. Though larger industry research indicates this age group represents a smaller percentage of all RVers, data also shows that their numbers are climbing. It's refreshing to see growth in this demographic as it's younger RVers who will continue to sustain this lifestyle as the older generations hang up their keys."*

Whether or not you'll work is a subject that will need research and planning. If you're considering working while you travel, some excellent websites cater to itinerant job seekers, such as Happy Vagabonds [3] and Workamper News [4] These websites connect employers with a seasonal mobile workforce as needed. Amazon's CamperForce [5] actively recruits RVers at some of its warehouse distribution centers. The company hires seasonally and offers a competitive wage, some benefits and a monthly allowance for campground fees.

If volunteering is more your style, there are a variety of opportunities to volunteer as you travel. You could work on a team to build a home for Habitat for Humanity [6], support a church camp, lend a hand at a political campaign office or help out at an animal rescue location. Whatever your interest or passion, there is opportunity everywhere for connections where you can make a difference, becoming part of a community in the process.

It would only be natural for you to have some angst about re-engineering your life to full-time travel living. You'll be making a physical move similar to moving out of one apartment to another. At the same time, you'll be changing your neighborhood. It's a lot of work and it'll trigger a whole range of emotions. You may run the gamut between nostalgia for what you're leaving and joy for your new direction. If you take the time to tune into your emotions and thoughts about this transition, you'll move forward with your plans with higher purpose and ease. Cultivate curiosity about the fact that this turning point in your life holds yet undiscovered treasures.

[1] http://tolkiengateway.net/wiki/The_Riddle_of_Strider

[2] https://www.escapees.com/

[3] https://www.happyvagabonds.com/Jobs/Jobs-By-State.htm

[4] https://workamper.com/

[5] https://www.amazondelivers.jobs/about/camperforce/

[6] https://www.habitat.org/

Chapter Two
What is Mobile Community?

Coddiwomple; to travel purposefully towards an as yet unknown destination
(kod'e wom pel)

The hardest part of writing a book about mobile community might just be coming up with a current working definition. While there are traditional ways in which we think about the concept, actually boiling it down to a specific meaning that applies in today's evolving world is tricky.

No matter where you reside today, you have access to a variety of groups of shared interests. The groups that you belong to today aren't static. They will shift and change over time. Today you belong to a parenting group focused on small children and later in life, you may belong to a caregiver support group for aging parents. In between, you may join a church family, a ski club, enjoy books with a reading group, or raise and show a favorite breed of dog with other enthusiasts. You're a core member of some and an occasional participant in others. No matter the focus of the group, you will seek different satisfactions from all of them.

Connecting with Others

Most of my life has been spent thinking about, teaching and working to build community-based networks for a variety of people. In my early career, I worked in social services on behalf of citizens who belonged to marginalized populations. The agency served children in foster care, refugees and citizens with developmental disabilities, elderly folks and others who did not enjoy full inclusion in their communities. I've had a lifelong interest in how people belong, how the sense of connection comes into being and how to sustain it. So, I recognize the challenges that face travelers to acquire a real sense of belonging, fellowship and connection as they move about the country in homes on wheels leaving behind what is familiar.

To explore this challenge, I set out to talk with as many people as possible about how they experienced their transition to mobile living. I knew that there was only one way to provide any compelling information to people who are considering RVing full-time. I would need to be out in the field, collecting stories and interviewing folks who are doing it. Their thoughts and feelings about this lifestyle are inspiring. And I appreciated their willingness to share their stories.

Over three years and in a series of just over one-hundred interviews with solos, couples, families and groups, I discovered a multitude of reasons that people answer the call of the road. People told of the labors, struggles, challenges, triumphs and rewards of living this lifestyle. All their stories were unique, but there were also common themes. Some were committed hodophiles, full-time lovers of the road. Some were seeking a *dérive*, a spontaneous journey where the traveler leaves their life behind to let the spirit of the land attract and move them. Other themes also wove through the interviews, but as a picture began to emerge, it became clear that no matter the underlying motivation, this is a major life transition with pros and cons for nearly everyone who chooses it.

Root Communities

In the majority of the interviews, people began by talking about something that I've come to call their *root community*. In answer to the age-old question, "Where are you from originally?" nearly everyone told a story about where they grew up or the specific location that they call their home base. In other words, they began with geography. If you want to know where you're going, it's helpful to see where you've been. So, let's have a look at the concept of root community and why it's vital to understanding the idea of mobile community.

Our *root communities* are more than just geography. They are also the people we share geography with; those with whom we hold trusting relationships. They are who we turn to in good times and bad. It might be virtual, online, or in-person. When discussing their root community, folks spoke of groups that they belong to, such as extended family, ethnic affiliations, neighborhoods, religious congregations, sports clubs, political alignments, online special interest groups, music and other fan groups. These geographic and specific interest connections make up your unique root community.

Many root communities are quite homogenous and prone to group think. [1] Journalist Bill Bishop is the author of *The Big Sort; Why the Clustering of Like-Minded America Is Tearing Us Apart.* [2] At the Aspen Ideas Festival, he said, "It used to be that people were born as part of a community and had to find their place as individuals. Now people are born as individuals and have to find their community." Bishop analyzes big picture demographics to show how American communities are sorting themselves at all levels into groups who hold strongly shared common values.

But the collection of people who travel is the antithesis of group-think. It is, by its very nature, diverse in geographic origin, political persuasion, religious affiliation, age, race and gender. It consists of folks who have left mostly homogenous and familiar communities to join one that's wholly different than what they have known. For some who are new to the lifestyle, this shift will ask them to step out of their comfort zone and into contact with people and places that are foreign to them. This transition is smooth for some and for others, it can be rather unsettling.

Are you wondering how you'll find your comfort zone without a home base? If so, you're not alone. Perhaps we might start by rethinking our concept of what constitutes community overall and from that develop a broader understanding that is a better fit with mobile circumstances.

Your Invested Roots

A sense of belonging is a universal longing. Whether home base was rural Virginia, a suburb of Chicago, a condo in Miami, or a fishing village in Maine, people spoke of their home as that place that held strong emotion. I interviewed a gentleman by the name of Nelson, who told me about the high personal investment he had while serving in his hometown as a selectman. He'd been in this position for twenty-one years. Nelson was the repository of so much history and continuity that leaving was wrenching for him. It was hard for the folks he served with too.

"I didn't know what they were going to do when I left. I always answered all the questions and no one ever had to go look anything up because I had it all up here." He pointed to his head. "But it was time for someone younger to step up. My wife finally convinced me that no one is indispensable, so I didn't run that last year." He chuckled. "But they still call me and I still answer the phone."

When we make a personal connection to our home town like Nelson, we're invested in it. We care about how to sustain the place that we live and value. I heard stories from teachers, business owners, Elk lodge members, food bank staff, animal rescue non-profits and many more. Each person was interested in some aspect of their root community that meant something special to them. Through their charitable and civic service, they gained a sense of belonging and ownership that enriched their lives.

If you've been an active participant like Nelson, your contribution to your home town is a part of its ongoing creation. Maybe you served on a non-profit board, coached little league, or fund-raised for a family undergoing a health crisis. Perhaps you donated to a new ball field, lobbied for parking improvements, planted flowers in a common area, or worked on the master plan for the school system. Maybe you sang in a church choir or participated in an annual beach clean-up. These are the concepts, actions and activities that bind people to their communities through a strong sense of belonging. Our root communities have robust legitimate ties and the thought of leaving these roots is something that can give prospective wanderers pause.

Creating Wings from Roots

Consider this: you have your roots; now you need to grow those wings. It's time to take all of the knowledge and skills that you've learned from your root community and translate them into building a new mobile community for yourself.

The transition is a journey of self-discovery. This marvelous adventure is going to challenge you to reflect upon the existing relationships you value and your place in the world. Dr. Dieter Duhm [3] writes eloquently on the subject of the goal of our life's journey in his blog post entitled, Is There a Humane Universe? He says, "The world which we create and the world which created us have come together. This is the goal of the journey." It's also true of the journey upon which you're about to embark. Just as your familiar root community is one that you've created, the world that you're about to discover will create you all over again. Belonging to the world of travelers is a transformative experience.

One of the questions that I tried to ask in each interview was, "Did your strong roots give you wings?" In other words, did the strength of your roots give you the curiosity and courage to make a change in what and where you call home? That was surely the case for Arnie and me. For many of the folks I've interviewed, the answer is also a definite yes. Although leaving home was, in some instances wrenching, paradoxically, the strength to go came from the quality of the ties to our original home itself.

Geographic Roots

How will you take the skills and values gained from where you lived and translate them into a mobile lifestyle? It will take a shift in thinking since your concept of community will no longer be about living on that cul-de-sac with a clear sense of neighborhood. Up until fourth grade, I lived in a tiny mill town in rural New Hampshire called Beebe River. [4] It was an experimental town conceived on the model of a utopian village. Beebe River was a microcosm of community sustainability where all the needs of the residents were present in the town itself. It was built in 1917 and taken over by the Draper Corporation in 1925. Draper continued the model as it had in its original experiment in utopian living in the mill town of Hopedale, Massachusetts. [5]

New England mill towns provided workers and their families with more than just company housing and factory jobs. A quintessential storekeeper by the name of Solly Tashjian and his wife Lil, ran the company store and Post Office. Their store stocked meat and groceries, clothing, shoes, boots, hunting supplies and nearly all the necessities of everyday life. These were the days where everyone in the town ran a tab until Friday payday and then came in and paid Solly in cash. If they didn't, they answered to Lil.

Beebe boasted a large recreation hall run by Draper Corporation, where plays, music concerts, birthday parties, company picnics, etc. took place. The village provided garden space in the upper field and softball teams from neighboring towns came down to Beebe to compete against the town team in the lower field. The two-room schoolhouse educated the children and the nurse's office tended to sick kids and mill accidents. My grandfather, fondly known as Barta, was the Office Manager, my grand-mother, Mamie, worked as a bookkeeper, my mother was the RN in the nurse's office and Dad worked in the mill. All needs were met within the town, so people seldom ventured far.

There was a strong sense of belonging and communal responsibility. The eyes of the village oversaw every child, especially when we were wayward. If some lady in that town told you to blow your nose, you took the tissue she handed you and blew your nose. We'd never even think of smarting off to our elders. At least not within hearing distance.

The town is nearly gone now; buildings have collapsed in ruin and the remnants are decaying. Very few of the older folks who lived in Beebe River when I was growing up would have been able to imagine a mobile lifestyle. A scenario in which they chose to leave the familiarity of their cohesive root community in favor of living in an RV would have been quite a puzzling concept to them.

Despite the disappearance of the physical village, Beebe Rivers' sense of identity was so binding that it endures today sixty years later in the form of a Facebook page. To this day, the former children of this vibrant mill town enjoy chatting online and exchanging what we remember about growing up. Many have dug deep into closets to retrieve old family photos to post on the page. The strong sense of belonging continues to act as the glue to this geographic place that binds us fondly together across the miles and the years. Although we've physically moved on, we still value the common emotional ties and memories that we shared.

And it's fascinating to me to know that a significant percentage of the children who grew up in the village of Beebe River enjoy camping and extensive traveling today. We may no longer have the fields of this small town to meet in, but we have a wider world to share and with technology we can stay in touch and share photos and stories of our travel adventures. When possible, we plan for our paths to cross and we meet up along the way to share time in a campground and reconnect in person.

There are numerous ways to keep strong ties after you are no longer geographically close to those you care about. If you are concerned about leaving behind friends and loved ones, be comforted by the fact that it does not have to be all or nothing. You can Skype with your grandchildren, receive the church newsletter through email and stay in touch with friends easily via smartphone.

Career Identities

In addition to our geographical home bases and communities of shared interests, when we adopt a nomadic lifestyle, we're often leaving behind careers and workplace relationships. Whether we're retiring or departing our workplace to home-school our children from an RV, we'll be leaving behind another source of belonging and identity. Our workplaces have often been where we engaged with others around shared goals and fulfilled our need for belonging. As you consider traveling full time, you may wonder what it will be like to disengage from your career and the close associations that you've built at work.

In my second career in the field of Community Association Management in South Florida, I became part of a business group focused on fostering successful residential associations. In an ever-changing business environment, we had responsibility for both the business and the human side of shared residential communities. As excited as I was for retirement, it was hard to imagine leaving behind my work. I'd need to part with my association boards, my workplace relationships and all of the trappings of a professional career I'd accomplished to reach for the dream of living full time in an RV.

Some people that I interviewed had no trouble on a social level leaving their workplace because it did not represent a robust interpersonal tie for them. Yet other aspects of leaving that career situation caused anxiety. One such person, Erica, told me that she was ready to go when the time came. "I knew that I had to quit the job that I'd been at for four years. I'd been unhappy and hated going to work. Leaving was the best thing I could do to kick-start a change even though I had some fear and con-cerns. I always knew that there were exciting things I wanted to do, but I was a single woman in my fifties. I was kind of afraid to leave. I thought maybe I lacked what it takes to make a go of my own business. But what was I going to do? Should I suck it up and stay where I was because that's what I know?" Erica ex-plained that she stayed on at her old job for a four-month transition period while she set up a consulting business that she could do from the road. She left to wander in 2012 and now visits children and grandchildren who are scattered coast to coast. "I can't believe I waited so long. I'm using my degree and all the skills I accumulated over the years to help non-profits. I have enough work to live on and be comfortable. Who needs more?"

Erica travels solo and I was interested in what that experience is like for her. When I asked her about a sense of belonging, Erica explained that she was very methodical. "I didn't want to take a blind leap and find myself with no connections or supports."

She kept up all of her professional memberships and she often visits along the way with other people in her field. "I still have my professional network. I just don't call them from an office anymore. I rely heavily on mobile technology and if I have a speaking gig, I park the RV and fly to where I need to go." She also joined a variety of groups that focus on women's adventure touring. "That's been a work in progress. Some groups I'll keep and some aren't as helpful. It's essential to me to be connected personally as well as professionally, so I do put effort into staying engaged with other people."

Blending Roots and Wings

Finding a way to blend into a new mobile community is something that most people think about when they travel full-time. Keeping tied to our original roots is another consideration. One couple who we met has pretty well figured out how to do both at the same time. We happened upon Rachael and Ben on a bluegrass afternoon in Kentucky. We noticed that they'd set up a small book exchange on their campsite with an inviting sign announcing, "Campfire Storytime. Please take a book and share it." Children and parents were popping by to choose a book and when they did, Rachael and Ben invited them to stop over at seven that evening for storytime and popcorn around the campfire. Of course, I just had to go over and chat with them to see what the backstory was.

They're both retired educators. Rachel is a bubbly dynamo of a lady who taught middle-school. Watching her with the kids who stopped by for books, it was easy to imagine her managing a classroom full of kids and making each one feel special. Ben is a quiet sort and his career was as a college professor teaching early childhood education at the University of Vermont. They were about five years into their retirement life on the road and we talked about how much they loved their lifestyle.

Campfire Stories is their creative solution and genius idea for continuing to serve children while preserving Ben and Rachel's connections to their own root community. Rachel explained, "From our teaching careers, we both had maintained valuable contacts. We knew we wanted to get books into the hands of kids. So, we enlisted the help of friends and associates from the book world that we knew back when we were teaching. They keep us supplied with samples of the latest children's literature. Books are shipped ahead to us along our itinerary to keep the weight in the RV down and free up space." Colleagues from Ben's college and Rachael's school send books too.

Ben chimed in. "We seek out yard sales, library book sales and thrift stores because they're a prolific source of outgrown children's books. We find books that are brand new and still in excellent condition. It's like a treasure hunt." We agreed that I'd drop by for storytime and then stay for a drink afterward. I couldn't wait to hear more.

After a delightful sharing of the fire and story with eight youngsters in attendance, I settled in to hear more about Rachael and Ben's journey. Rachael and Ben are connecting with young readers all across the country. They're gifting not only books but sparking curiosity and conversation around a campfire with children and parents. Rachel spoke to the benefits that they derive from their endeavor.

"This project keeps us connected to colleagues and the world of teaching that was our life. By contributing books to our project, our friends feel a part of our travels and we continue to maintain valuable relationships that took years to develop."

Soft-spoken Ben stirred the fire and added his perspective of a proud grandpa. "The best thing about this is that our grandchildren are tied into the project too. When there is good Wi-Fi, we do Facetime with them during the campfire story hour. Sometimes, granddaughter Nicole, who wants to be a teacher, is the guest reader. Other times they listen in with the other children. Our grandson Jacob is our extrovert; he enjoys talking with some of the children who are home-schooling and traveling. Right now, he's doing a joint project on hawks with another boy his age and we hope they will meet in person one day."

I asked Rachael where the idea originated. "Two years into our travels, we began to feel a sense of drifting. We'd decompressed from careers and crisscrossed the US seeing many of our bucket list places. We were nowhere near ready to give up our RV lifestyle, but we were beginning to long for something outside of ourselves. That's when we came up with Campfire Stories. It's given us a purpose. It's been a godsend to us and we know the kids love it too. As a hidden agenda to the actual reading of the story, we try to work in some talk about conservation ethics, appreciation and preservation of nature, whatever we can relate to the story. So, we use a format where we read and then discuss the book. That gets the parents involved too. Sometimes it gets pretty lively."

Ben explained that they sometimes request Ranger participation if appropriate. "We always call ahead to check with every campground to ask permission. We're now getting requests for return engagements."

Rachael and Ben's work is a perfect example of traveling with a purpose. These two delightful people are sharing their fire and giving young readers a unique travel experience too.

Your Membership in the Mobile Community

The moment you begin to travel on the road, you have actually established yourself as a member of the mobile community.

Without realizing it, you will have banded together with a collection of people who have these things in common:

- We are curious and share a mindset of discontent that leads us to want to live a mobile lifestyle.

- We are in the process of wrestling with essential questions about how to find a full and soulful life when our home base is being redefined every day as we travel

- We have questions and considerations regarding our vehicles and roadways and other RV-related circumstances that the land-bound don't encounter.

The band of brothers and sisters who share the road full-time has a tacit understanding that we share these concerns. We share tools, skills, time and expertise because we understand that knowledge is key to a successful experience on the road. We learn from each other and rely on each other. No matter how much we think we know, we will need to develop an on-going and current expertise about all aspects of full-time RVing. We need current opportunities to engage with others. Sharing valuable knowledge requires interaction and informal learning processes such as storytelling, conversation and coaching.

As you meet people, you will gain personal satisfaction in knowing RVing colleagues who understand each other's perspectives. It will be rewarding and enjoyable to belong to such an exciting group of people. Over time, this group has developed a shared sense of identity based on sharing much more than just a fire. Because of the collective nature of knowledge, we need others to complement and expand our expertise.

While a community identity for wanderers is admittedly thorny to pin down, there is still a common inborn desire to connect even when that connection is fluid. You will meet folks at all stages of life who are finding new solutions for the common problems that arise on the road. You will find your own ways to integrate into, contribute to and benefit from being a member of this unique and evolving network. Who will be your tribe?

[1] https://www.psychologytoday.com/us/basics/groupthink/5

[2] http://www.thebigsort.com/home.php

[3] https://www.dieter-duhm.com/2018/09/11/is-there-a-humane-subject-in-the-universe/

[4] http://www.camptonhistorical.org/beebe%20river%20marker%20flyer.pdf

[5] https://en.wikipedia.org/wiki/Hopedale_Community

Chapter Three
Is the Wandering Lifestyle Right for You?

"There is, in sanest hours, a consciousness, a thought that rises, independent,
lifted out from all else, calm, like the stars, shining eternal."
- Walt Whitman

It all begins with a nagging curiosity. Perhaps thoughts of what it would be like to live in an RV are beginning to arise during the day to day routine of your present life. Imaginings about how it would feel to call an RV home are beginning to intrude upon your mind during meetings, your morning commute and while you're washing the dishes. Maybe your neighbor has an RV in his yard, or perhaps you drive by an RV dealership each day on your way to work.

Something is rising inside you that needs to manifest itself. Its voice is making demands and asking you to heed the call of the road. The clamoring becomes persistent and impossible to ignore. More and more, you begin to wonder about what it would be like to be headed somewhere in that big fifth-wheel passing you on the Interstate. Is this merely a vagary, a wild, unusual idea or a desire for a wandering journey? Is it an unpredictable longing filled with whimsy, or is this the beginning of a serious life change?

Before you know it, that initial curiosity is taking the shape of a dream that fills your inner consciousness. Repeatedly, people that Arnie and I meet tell us that living a nomadic life is their dream. Many also comment that they hear the siren call but lack the courage to break all that ties them into jobs, roles, or even self-image. Severing the umbilical cord of safety and tradition is a daunting exchange for living life as a rough draft. But still, they seem to feel that the conformist identify that they currently have may be totally at variance with the wilderness energies that are rising in their souls. The Germans refer to it as *fernweh*, a craving for travel, or being homesick for a place you've never been to. Do you long to become one of the traveling storytellers? If you never try out the wondering lifestyle, will you feel that you've settled for something familiar and safe? Will you regret missing the opportunity for adventure that is in your spirit?

Admittedly, that siren call is enticing and some of us are predisposed to impulsive life decisions. RVing has the mystique of being an idyllic lifestyle envied by many, but there are questions to ask yourself before you just put the truck in gear and wave goodbye in the rearview mirror.

Where to Start

So, where do you begin to think about whether or not the nomadic lifestyle would suit you? It can seem like a pretty overwhelming process. There is an old Chinese proverb that says: "Pearls don't lie on the seashore. If you want one, you must dive for it." Sure, there are some happy road trippers who just suddenly packed up and left home one day without a look back. For most of us, though, it takes planning and it takes work. But this part of the journey can be enjoyable and fun too. It will be up to you to decide how much time and effort you want to devote to preparations as opposed to just doing it. It's your unique adventure, so you are free to pick and choose the advice in this book that best fits your needs.

A great place to start is to find a quiet spot and time to let your imagination run free. There will be ample time later for reality to set in, but, to start, why not just indulge yourself in a bit of fantasy?

We met one young couple, Neil and Shelly, who had decided to capitalize on an unexpected situation and make lemonade from lemons. They had not given any serious thought to radically shifting their lifestyle until their jobs suddenly were eliminated at the same time. Neil and Shelly both worked for a moderate size start-up firm in the greater Boston area. Neil managed operations and Shelly was in HR. When the company was bought out, the new owners made a decision to bring in their own staff and the couple found themselves unemployed with little warning. It just so happened that their apartment lease was coming up for renewal that same month, so they quickly decided to turn in a different direction. They took over the payments on Shelly's parents' 2012 motorcoach and hit the road, workamping along the way. They are flexible people who saw an opening and stepped right into it with very little time to plan or prepare. The two are thriving and love life in the Bounder with their adopted German Shepherd mix, who is also named Bounder. Shelly summed up their sudden pivot. " It was a stressful time at first. We got bounded out our jobs, we adopted Bounder, the dog and we are now living in a Bounder motorcoach. What's not to love? It worked out great. " With little time to second guess themselves, Neil and Shelly embarked with a positive attitude that has taken them into a whole new life. These upbeat folks are proof that a transition that is accomplished quickly and under some pressure can still be satisfying and smooth.

We have met others who made successful short transitions, but for the most part, it takes planning and it takes work. The good news is that this part of the journey can be enjoyable and fun too. A great place to begin is to find a quiet spot and time to let your imagination run free. There will be ample time later for reality to set in but, to start, why not just indulge yourself in a bit of fantasy? Children's author and illustrator Maurice Sendek reminds us that "A wish is halfway to wherever you want to go."

Most of us live with a foot in two worlds; the world we currently inhabit and another beckoning world that we imagine is out there. The discomfort that we feel when we're in between two places is ripe with opportunity. It's fertile ground for growing and expanding our perspective, a much better garden for change than when we're satisfied and content with our circumstances.

Since few of us can live totally in the moment, much of our energy is spent thinking about how to create ways to bridge those two worlds. We've figured out how to step over from the life we are living into the life we think we want. To light the path across the bridge, we can ask ourselves illuminating questions. In this chapter, I'll help you explore those topics that'll shed light on a practical and central question, "Is the nomadic lifestyle for me?" I invite you to use the material in this chapter to start a dialogue with yourself, your traveling partner, or your family. Make it a discussion that will hone your decision-making and move your life in the direction of your dreams.

Brainstorming

There is value in taking the time to brainstorm with someone you trust. Talk with a confidant who knows you well and can walk through your dreams and hopes for this adventurous life decision with you. Sit down and ruminate about how this is going to roll out. Write down all of your thoughts and concerns together, no matter how wild and crazy they may be. You can whittle it down later. For now, it's essential to get everything down in black and white. Just capture your thought process as you examine the positives and negatives in the company of a valued listener.

Post-it-Notes are a great planning tool. Dedicate a wall in your home office as a dream wall. Leave it up where you can see the evolution of your thought process every day and make adjustments as you continue to think yourself in the direction of a decision. My first Post-it list started on the refrigerator and later, as it grew, it moved to our dream wall. The list was funny, irreverent and reflective of my longing to find a way to leave the crazy corporate world. I was very aware that I had a lot to learn about full-time RVing and much to consider in getting to that point in life.

As Confucius counseled, "Real knowledge is to know the extent of one's ignorance." I knew I had much knowledge to acquire and this initial list helped me to target those areas where I lacked knowledge or insight. The list included dream destinations as well as notes reflective of the frustration of working in a high-stress job. I began to be able to see in black and white some excellent reasons why I wanted to change lifestyles. The pros and cons changed and evolved over two years, while I continued to work towards retirement.

Having the brainstorming list in such a prominent place eventually engaged my husband and it became a fun mutual planning tool. It created excitement and anticipation as it evolved from a loose collection of thoughts to actual goals and desires for our life on the road. As retirement got close, Arnie and I were very ready for real change, not just the rearranging furniture kind of change. But before we upended life as we knew it, we felt a real responsibility to examine the reasons we wanted to make a change. We thought it was essential to be sure that we were thinking about RVing realistically and for all the right reasons. We didn't want to initiate change just for the sake of change.

Defining the Big Picture

We concentrated next on defining the big picture. We pulled down the Post-It Notes with the questions and comments that reflected our more existential fears and expectations, compiled them into a list and started the serious discussion here. These were the deep questions that we wanted to ask. They were designed to help us think about whether giving up our home and living full-time in an RV would suit us. Nuts and bolts would come later. More than any other exercise, this one brought Arnie and me closer together in our quest. Of course, we didn't answer the existential questions (who can?). However, we did use them to explore how we'd share another phase of life that would be very different than the one we'd been living. I recommend that you set aside some time to sit down and examine these questions with your traveling partner or a trusted friend if you plan to travel solo. This discussion will be sure to uncover some useful insights for you.

- How do you measure life?

- Is this decision part of your purpose?

- When you look at everything that's taken place in your life up until now, did it lead to this?

- What do you want to be a part of?

- Where do you find meaning in life?

- How do you know you are doing the right thing?

Practical Considerations

After we looked at the big picture, we turned our attention to the practical considerations we had put up on our dream wall. It was time to look at the nuts and bolts. Following a series of evolutions, that list had eventually whittled itself down to reality. Maybe some of these questions will fit your situation and help you to polish your thought process.

- Should you keep your home? What are all of the financial considerations and ramifications of not keeping a home base?

- Do you know exactly what you spend now and what you can expect to spend when you turn the key in the ignition and leave?

- Do you have the proper vehicle and equipment already and if not, what changes need to happen? Will you be traveling mostly highways or back roads? Mountain routes or flatter terrain?

- Can you afford this? Are you willing to tighten the belt now and make sure you can live within an RVing budget with accommodation for emergencies?

- Will you need to continue to work full or part-time? If so, what kind of job could you do?

- Should you go completely "stuff free" or keep a few things in storage while you travel?

- What about healthcare? Does your current insurance plan accommodate travel, or is it regional only? What are the options?

- No matter how much experience you have with recreational camping, there is a learning curve about full-time living in an RV. How will you evaluate what you need to learn and acquire that information from reliable sources?

- What about your pets? Will they be comfortable with continuous change? Can you accommodate their unique needs?

- What mobile technology will you need on board to help you maintain your ties to friends and family?

- Do you want to ease into the lifestyle part-time or take the leap to full-time?

- What are some of the destinations that most interest you?

- Are you most comfortable staying in one place for extended visits, or would you prefer to move around frequently?

- Do you find the thought of staying in an urban area at a five-star RV resort appealing, or are you more of a wilderness lover?

- Will you want to connect with other like-minded people by camping with groups or, are you set on getting away from civilization and charting your solo course for a while?

As you work your way through all the things to consider, the planning process will move you forward. You'll graduate from dreaming to planning by taking the time to evaluate your questions, thoughts and ideas about a nomadic lifestyle. Clarity will begin to emerge out of the creative chaos and a target date with some steps for getting there will develop. Finally, you'll have a decision and a plan. You'll be well on your way to transitioning into being a member of the wandering community.

Like most couples, Arnie and I didn't always agree on everything during our transition to RVing. But we did use this process to provide a guide for mutual decision making. We could visually see where we shared ideas and where we weren't on the same page. Our likes and dislikes were right there in black and white in front of us. We took the time and cared enough to be sure that both of us were comfortable with the final decision. This process takes lots of communication, compromise and a good deal of patience, but it's worth all of the effort it takes to do it together.

There was one other helpful exercise that we used to get on the same page. Since we were both leaving corporate worlds focused on specific missions, we were familiar with using mission statements to guide our work. Why not use one to guide our wandering? We hoped it would serve as a handy reminder of our original purpose and give us a bit of inspiration on those days when the going gets tough. It seemed like a simple introspective exercise at the time that we composed it, but it indeed has been a valuable base to return to time and again. We've used it to stay on mission and not get side-tracked from what we want to see and experience. If you're interested in writing a mission state-ment, consider reading *The Path, Creating Your Mission Statement for Work and Life* by Laurie Beth Jones. [1] After a bit of trial and error, we created the following:

> *"Our mission for our travel is to be respectful, mindful and present with each person, place and creature that we encounter, to keep an open and learning mindset and always be a welcoming refuge of compassion, kindness and wellness to all who chose to share our fire."*

You might be wondering about timing. Perhaps your planning is well underway by now and you're wondering when you should finally heed that eccentric inner voice. When should you nudge the door to the garden wide open and stroll through it and what's keeping it closed right now? Undoubtedly, dismantling one season of life to be able to embark on the next one isn't simple. At the same time, there is no denying that life is both precious and transient. Maybe we'll live with good health to a ripe old age and maybe not. Will there ever really be an entirely right time for you to start your journey and the potential for joy that it will hold for you? Timing is an individual decision and you'll move closer to an answer to this question as you continue to plan for your travels.

Dan and Marlene have been on the road for 26 years now. I met them first in Alabama at an Army Corps of Engineers campground along the Alabama River Lakes. For them, the right time to embark on their wanderings came earlier than for many folks. Dan took early retirement in his mid-fifties from his job back in the days when factory work came with a pension. Marlene had worked in a physician's practice managing the business and also had savings. With kids finally launched and funds in place, they made careful plans to transition to RVing. After attending to all of the details, they sold their home, loaded their fifth wheel and never looked back.

Dan and Marlene travel the country with purpose in the company of a group of like-minded volunteers. As they move from place to place, they help out with projects at non-profits in exchange for a free site and hookups. They could've continued to work for many years, but chose instead to start their nomadic life relatively young. They joined a group called Sowers [2] and have enjoyed sharing their values and faith while helping out non-profits that have a mission to assist Christian ministries. Their group works on projects needed by camps, schools, children's homes, retreat centers, recovery homes, etc., located throughout the continental United States as well as some in Canada. It's become their mission, purpose and way of life. "We weren't escaping from anything when we made our decision to go full time. Instead, we felt as if we were always traveling towards something meaningful." Marlene shared.

They live frugally and have crisscrossed the country dozens of times, making a contribution where needed and living an exciting life. The projects served by Sowers provide all hookups, mitigating the expenses of the volunteers to some extent. They have no regrets that they timed their lifestyle change early. Although the couple is now in their late seventies, they have no plan to settle down any time soon. It was clear from talking with Dan and Marlene that they're living their very best lives.

Marlene explained what she loves about their traveling lives. "We've been blessed to be able to work shoulder to shoulder with people that we would never have met if we had stayed in our hometown in New York. We go to volunteer sites for three weeks at a minimum and that gives us enough time to feel a real part of the group we're with. Often we schedule volunteer gigs so that some of our favorite friends from past projects can be together again for a time. We're a group of service-minded people who like being with other service-minded people and we enjoy making a difference."

Dan added another thought about timing. He shared that their kids think that it's time for them to make another change and they'd like to see their parents return home. "They want us to come home and be old where they can take care of us, but we're just not ready. We don't feel old. Besides, as much as I love them, I don't want to babysit the great-grandkids. I know the kids worry a lot, but I still have lots to give and they'll have to pry my hands off that steering wheel until I'm ready."

I asked whether they had any concerns about aging and traveling full time. Both Dan and Marlene have dealt with health crises during their travels. Marlene shared some wisdom. "You have to be prepared to deal with whatever comes in place. Where you are is where you solve it. We go home once a year to our primary doctor for routine stuff and the rest of the time, we use some good old-fashioned common sense." Dan chimed in, "We keep good insurance and we don't take crazy risks...anymore anyway. We used to climb higher mountains, drive a bit further each day and work on more taxing projects. Now we know our limits and abide by them." I had to chuckle because I'd seen him climbing down from the ladder he was using to clean off the roof of the fifth wheel. Let's not tell the kids.

Arnie and I were in our mid-sixties when we made our decision. The world was calling out to us and we were longing to hear its voice. We were ready to restore legitimacy to our lives through a connection to nature and a penchant for learning. But we understood that this life wasn't just carefree. During the planning stages, we tried to be brutally honest with ourselves and with each other. We wanted to determine if the tradeoff between the travel we longed for and the realities of a full time traveling life were worth it to us. We needed to be sure that we weren't just tired and burned out from years of high-stress jobs. We needed to be sure that we weren't just looking for an escape. We also needed to know that we were dreaming of a fulfilling lifestyle that would be realistic for us to execute. We asked ourselves if this was the right lifestyle and the right decision at the right time for us. Jumping from the frying pan into the fire may be tempting, but long term, you'll probably get burned. Ultimately, we decided to fine-tune the plan and then put it in action.

As we worked on a grand design for the template of a new and exciting life, we had to remind ourselves not to cling too tightly to it. As lifelong big-picture planners, we now would also need to build flexibility and spontaneity into the plan. We sensed that if we clung too tightly to a rigid template of what we wanted life on the road to look like, we'd commit ourselves to a narrow experience of it. We decided that it made sense for us to plan our trips out ahead, mapping the route and identifying what we wanted to see along the way. By infusing planning with flexibility, we'd be relaxed and present enough to enjoy the journey. We knew there would be some wrong turns, back roads and detours along the way, so we planned to take my dad's sage advice. "If you skid off course, don't slow down."

We have met folks from all walks of life who found their own balance of planning and spontaneity that worked perfectly for them. There are no hard and fast rules for this, only the good experience of others to draw upon as you find what works best for you. Going through the process of exploring whether the mobile lifestyle is for you is a process of self-discovery. It's the first of many discoveries you'll make about yourself as you prepare to take those wrong turns, back roads and detours.

[1] https://www.goodreads.com/book/show/462310.The_Path

[2] https://www.sowers.org/

Chapter Four
Family Matters

"Your family is your needs answered. Family is your field which you sow with love and reap with thanksgiving. When your family speaks their mind you fear not the 'nay' in your own mind, nor do you withhold the 'ay'."
- unknown

When we decide to reengineer our lifestyle there may be consequences for others who have little or no say in the decision making. Those effected may be spouses, children, parents and friends. There are ways to include those who love us and have our best interests in mind while still keeping that final decision ours.

If you can create alignment among those people that your decision will effect, you will be able to move forward with more confidence and less guilt. This does not mean that everyone will be in agreement, but your goal is to be sure that those who are effected have knowledge and understanding of what has led you to consider full-time travel.

Try to put yourself in the shoes of each person who will be impacted by your decision to RV full-time. Ask yourself if you would want them to allow you to weigh in with feelings and opinions if the roles were reversed. It is possible to balance your needs with the people you love and you can give each person a chance to have their voice heard even if your ultimate decision goes counter to their wishes. This is a time that may rewrite the legacy of you and also your family. Therefore, it is wise to let them have a say and to practice patience and empathy while you hear their contribution.

There is plenty of excitement and anticipation around the decision you are contemplating and it is easy to get caught up in the emotion and newness of RVing. Family and friends can help us think about the long term picture. Keep in mind though; your loved ones will be speaking with their own agendas and biases. Talk about that frankly and ask them to provide advice objectively based on how well they know you. The scariest part of making a monumental life change is that the decision you make ultimately is yours alone. It might be a good idea to think it through on your own and then present a coherent plan to them for their input.

Aligning with Your Spouse or Significant Other

My grandmother Mamie gave me some good advice about the marriage relationship. She said that there would be beautiful days and then there will be days that will try the patience of a saint. At the time, I thought she meant my patience, but now I think she may have been referring to my future husband who would have to put up with me. This advice is very pertinent to wandering in tandem with another person. Getting on the same page can, at times, try the patience of a saint. Ask Arnie.

Thankfully my dear husband shares this madness for travel handed down to me by nature and nurture from a family who all loved a trip and an adventure. Arnie and I work hard to stay in reasonable agreement with travel decisions and make them mutually because we know well that this lifestyle takes a lot of negotiation and diplomacy. We practice separation of duties according to our respective skill sets and regardless of traditional gender roles. Arnie plans the route and I navigate. He drives the truck and camper forward and I back it up. He does the outside maintenance and I keep the inside ship shape. We both wait hand and foot on the elderly dog, attending to her every whim and need. We do try to share the load equally whenever possible and do our best to talk through decisions mutually. From the very beginning, we pledged to work hard to be on the same page about where and when to travel.

But we've sadly talked with many spouses who went along with their better halves' lust for the road, only to be miserable. They underestimated how they'd feel about being separated from everything familiar. They missed their root community with its comforting ties to family and friends. For some folks, it wasn't possible to anticipate that anxieties would be more challenging to manage within the looser parameters of traveling. One lady, who's been on the road for just six months, told me that it was the biggest mistake she ever made. She explained that she's always been a nervous passenger, even in a car. Riding with the forty foot RV in tow had escalated her anxiety to an unbearable level. She acutely missed her home and her daughter and grandchildren. I felt such compassion for her as she shared that they had sold everything they owned to pursue what was her husband's retirement dream, but she's now miserably unhappy. As pleasant as wandering is for some, not everyone is equally keen on it.

What if your significant other isn't entirely convinced or ready to depart? Perhaps they have concerns or reservations? If your partner isn't showing the same eagerness and enthusiasm for travel like you, now is the time to sit down and enter into a fair discussion that addresses all of their questions and concerns. Take the time to wrestle together with some of the big-picture questions that we're exploring here. There is probably no other more critical time in the history of your relationship, be it short or long, for you to match your pace to one another. You're making a significant life transition and haste isn't your friend. If one of you is in the clutches of the wanderlust, it's best to practice restraint, diplomacy and tact while you allow your traveling partner to catch up. Through the process of doing your research and planning together, you'll be better able to meet in the middle and launch your life transition to full-timing more comfortably together.

There will still always be bumps in the road. This nomadic life calls us to be flexible and to roll with the punches. But open discussion with your traveling companion about wishes, needs, skills and lingering reservations before embarking will pave the way to a more successful experience.

Taking into Account Aging Parents

If you happen to have elderly parents there is another whole layer to your decision to go RVing. If this is not the right time for you to leave because you are responsible for other people, you can remind yourself that patience is a virtue. Maybe your decision cannot be made tomorrow, but you can persevere with your planning. Keep moving forward towards the day that it will be possible to realize your dream lifestyle.

Guilt is a powerful emotion and when we are away from elderly parents, it can rise to the surface easily. But guilt doesn't necessarily signal that you have made a bad choice. Perhaps you have just found the courage and strength to do what is best even when others are not on board with our decision. Maybe you are setting some necessary limits and moving forward with taking good care of yourself. If you make a decision that differs from what your family would have preferred, help them to understand why that decision was made. Take the time to explain with patience and empathy and they might be more likely to get on board with the adventure.

Convincing the Kids

When Arnie and I announced our plans to RV full time, our kids had some reservations. It was a surprise to us how the roles had reversed. Now we would be out of touch for longer periods of time while our exact whereabouts were unknown to them. We could have thought of this as revenge for their teenage years, but we really understood that they had legitimate concerns. We did want to be compassionate and not cause anyone undue worry.

For the most part, RVing is a very safe lifestyle when proper precautions are taken. But it is a complicated world and sometimes bad things occur. During the final days of writing this book, a tragic situation happened to a traveling couple from Arnie's hometown in New Hampshire. Jim and Michele Butler were boondocking in Texas and tragically lost their lives under suspicious circumstances. Their homicide had devastating consequences for their children, extended family and friends in their small community. As of this writing, it is unclear what happened, but it is a precautionary tale and we owe it to our adult children to be safety-minded while traveling. Listen to the concerns of your loved ones and make any adjustments that are practical to help them be as comfortable as possible with your decision to live mobile.

Being separated from loved ones for long periods was initially difficult for me to imagine. But with email, social media and Facetime we are never out of touch. When we have good Wi-Fi connection, we really enjoy video calls and seeing our kids and grandkids in their homes. We try to incorporate visits in our itinerary and also enjoy camping with the kids when we are in their locale. Yes, we have missed some special occasions, but we try hard to plan our travels to be present for the bigger one-time events such as weddings or the birth of a grandchild. Sickness or a death in the family cannot be anticipated, but we can always fly home as needed.

We do the very best we can to travel with safety in mind and to be aware and fully conscious of our surroundings. Finding a balance between taking prudent precautions and enjoying the freedom associated with RVing is a challenge that is important to master.

Considering Your Pets

A good friend once asked me a fair question. Have you two lost your minds traveling in a small space with all of those animals? I do admit that traveling in an RV with multiple animals calls us to a higher consciousness in many ways. After all, they are family members too and they did not get a vote in this decision to RV full-time.

We travel with a full house and it was a monumental undertaking to plan well so that they would be safe and comfortable along the journey. One of them is a diva, one is a socialite, and one likes to bite, so each presented us with a unique set of special needs. But like all who wander with their pets, we value their companionship and love being with them.

Our Japanese Chin, Hana, is an introvert and a diva. Traveling is not her chosen lifestyle and she has an obvious disdain for camping. When asked if she wants to go for a ride, Hana averts her gaze and grumbles under her breath like a snotty teenager with attitude. God forbid we should ask her to go outside if the grass is wet. Pollen makes her sneeze and hiking makes her wheeze. Her clearly expressed aversion to camping life has brought us a lot of laughs. But once we reach our destination, she is delighted to get out outside in her familiar portable pen. She barks a greeting to passersby, trying to get people to stop by and give her the attention due a drama queen.

Our little terrier, Wicca, on the other hand, is the extrovert and is at home in her skin in any situation. Wherever she goes, there she is. She makes friends of all people without prejudice, wagging a warm welcome to anyone who'll meet her eye. She's hospitality personified and draws people to our campsite with her enthusiasm for meeting new souls. Wicca has been an ambassador for us and facilitated by her great cuteness and outgoing personality, we've met and struck up conversations with lots of friendly people. These two exact canine opposites remind us that there is a place for both the introverts and the extroverts in our traveling communities. Their differences are valued.

We also journey with a finicky rescued African Grey Parrot who's become a seasoned happy traveler. Cracker is an amalgamation of quirks that make him a unique personality. If you've ever known a bird of this species, you're aware that they approach life from a cautious, suspicious point of view. They're wary by nature and don't dive into any experience without thinking it through and looking at the situation very carefully. African Greys generally like their environment to stay stable and secure and their routine to be predictable.

They're also known to be rigid, so it's pretty surprising how much Cracker likes to go places. He genuinely seems to enjoy watching us get his cage all set up and food packed. When we load his special car seat into the truck, Cracker chatters, "Let's go. You wanna go?" From the backseat, he comments on traffic by saying, "OWWEEE.", when large trucks pass by us. He wolf whistles at other drivers when we fill up with gas, causing more than a few offended stares at Arnie. He's like the annoying little brother in the backseat, repeating the dog's names over and over and telling them they're a "Good girl." and repeatedly asking, "Whatcha doin?"

We've encountered many people who are fascinated with birds and take them along as intelligent traveling companions. Cracker has been a great way to meet people who are curious about him, especially children. However, we try to educate everyone we meet about the pros and cons of acquiring any parrot as a pet; they're messy, loud and expensive to feed. Birds like Cracker are either captive bred or caught in the wild. In either case, life in a cage is unnatural and not in any way ideal. If you love birds and are considering traveling with one, contact a bird rescue group to learn how you can adopt an abused or neglected bird in need of a new home. Please don't add to the suffering by purchasing a bird from a pet store.

Cracker came to us quite by chance and not by choice and we're his guardians for this lifetime, responsible for his well-being in captivity. Because he can't fly free, we owe him the kindest and most compassionate circumstances that we can provide. Thus, his safety and comfort were considerations when we looked for a rig that would be the right fit. We consider him a beloved friend and companion and we respect his intelligence and his willingness to adapt to our moving about in different environments. No family is complete without a crazy uncle. Cracker is our crazy uncle who's along for the ride.

In the spring of 2018, we added another family member. Journey is an Entlebucher Mountain Dog, a rare breed that originated in Switzerland. For two years we had done careful research to narrow down our choice of a breed that would travel well and fit our needs. We attended dog shows, talked with breeders and met dozens of wonderful dogs. All of our other three pets were rescues, but this time we needed some specific characteristics if we were to successfully integrate another dog into our traveling circus. We needed a short-coated medium size breed with high intelligence and trainability. We were also looking for a breed that could offer some protection if needed.

Journey joined us as a rambunctious fourteen-week old puppy and she has lived up to her name. She grew up on the road while we worked hard to help her fulfill her purpose. Journey started her training right away with a professional trainer guiding us and all the work has paid off. At almost two now, she is my service dog and assists with tasks that make life on the road a bit easier. Her joyous upbeat personality will someday make her a great Therapy Dog when we visit libraries and nursing homes spreading her own brand of cheer. Journey holds multiple titles and certifications and she delights in being an ambassador for her breed. Since she was a very active puppy, we had to take her needs into consideration and provide socialization, stimulation and exercise on a daily basis just as we accommodated the needs of persnickety Hana and crazy old Cracker.

If you decide to share your travel adventures with pets, your experience will be richly enhanced by having them along. Pack up your babies and off you go like Neil Diamond's 1969 song *Brother Loves Traveling Salvation Show.*

Pack up the babies
And grab the old ladies
And everyone goes
'Cause everyone knows
Brother love's show.

It's Your Decision

Since we are human and to be human means to be in relationship, you will be challenged to take others' needs into consideration as you plan for your new mobile lifestyle. Now is the time to find your courage and create the life you want and deserve. It's not a popularity contest and you will never please everyone. At the end of the day, listen with consideration to the valued counsel of those who will be effected by your decision and then make a decision that you can live with for both the short and the long term.

Chapter Five
The Weight of Attachments

To free the chick,
The shell must be broken.
To free what is inside
One must shatter
What is outside.
- From The Lost Writings of Wu Ha

There are undeniable advantages to the RVing lifestyle. The ability to move about this beautiful country is freedom not given to all citizens of all nations. We should never take for granted the privilege that we enjoy to get behind the wheel of a vehicle and, for the most part, travel where the road takes us and see what we want to see with little obstruction to our choices. There is no more immediate way to learn about what makes America unique than to be there in person. But to realize this dream, most of us must examine the attachments that hinder living full-time on the road.

Letting go is not an easy process. In fact, there appears to be a biological explanation for why some folks find it extraordinarily challenging to part with belongings. Researchers at Yale School of Medicine conducted a study in 2013. [1] They recruited participants, some of whom were diagnosed with hoarding disorder and some who weren't. Researchers then asked them to sort through photos of junk mail and decide what to keep and what to toss. Some of the mail was their own and the researchers provided some pieces. During this activity, researchers tracked participants' brain activity on an MRI. Only the hoarders showed increased activity in two separate areas of the brain. The more that a hoarder reported feeling "not right" about parting with an item, the more pronounced this pattern of neural signature was. Both of these particular regions of the brain are associated with conflict and pain. You see the same pattern of brain activation in other areas of psychological discomfort, such as withdrawal from the cravings of smoking and drug addiction. Hoarding may be self-sustaining in that a person may experience a feeling of safety and calm when they hold onto something and that relief can become addictive.

Research gives insight into the fact that it's harder for some people than for others to part with items that provide them with comfort. People not diagnosed with hoarding disorder often still feel uncomfortable disposing of possessions. Is holding on to your belongings impeding your lifelong dream of travel? If so, it might be helpful to consider getting some professional help with making a plan for moving forward. NAPO is the National Association for Professional Organizers. NAPO will help you downsize and choose what items you want to keep, what you want to take with you in your RV and what you could eliminate. [2]

Owning a house isn't necessarily compatible with extensive travel. A lifetime of accumulated possessions weighs heavily on our mobility. Some people may be financially able to retain all their possessions and still travel full-time. But most folk's circumstances dictate that they will have to make some compromises to remove material impediments to allow for a mobile existence. RVing is, by necessity, a minimalist life in which collecting things is just not an option. Wrestling with attachment to our belongings is one of the preliminary steps that we all have to take in embarking on the RV lifestyle. We think that if we let go of something, we will lose something important. But in truth, we also gain something by letting go. By giving up possessions, we gain space, peace of mind and airiness that will be essential to transitioning to living in an RV.

The First Painful Detachment

My first difficult detachment came when I sold my small pick-up truck. I will never forget the wrench of parting with this much-loved vehicle to purchase one that had the proper capacity to pull our trailer. My little red Toyota Tacoma was the first brand-new vehicle I had ever bought as a single woman. I admit that I am slightly embarrassed at the very personal relationship I had with her. I was so proud of her; she was my girl truck and I named her *My Pretty Pony*. When I got her, she was volcanic red and maybe *Red Hot Mama* would have been a better name. But I didn't think I could live up to that nickname for all the years I intended to drive this vehicle. Also, I knew that my mother and her friend, who lived with me in Florida during the winter, would be driving the truck to bingo. I did not want people staring at two elderly ladies driving around in something I called Red Hot Mama. We all deserve our pathology and my unnatural attachment to this truck was mine.

Little did I know the adventures that truck and I would share. My Pretty Pony and I drove a kayak down to the sea and djembes to drum circles in the woods. She took me to scatter to rest the ashes of two beloved dogs high up in the Blue Ridge Mountains of Virginia along the Appalachian Trail. We ran out for milk together or to have a private cry when needed. She helped me move my belongings from house to house in joy and sadness. My truck sped me along as I sang out loud to the music on the way to Key West to visit my kids and the crowd went wild. We explored native Florida with camping gear piled high on her back. She was my Sherpa, my llama, my suitcase, my magic carpet and gypsy cart. When Arnie and I married, we took our first camping trip together with her pulling the load in her always reliable style. When it came time to sell her, my husband placed this ad on Craigslist:

This is a rare buy. This single owner vehicle belongs to my obsessive wife, who's pampered it for all its years. She's religiously changed the oil, maintained it like she might need to live in it someday and kept it hand waxed. She added running boards, an updated tow package, bed liner and fiberglass topper. God forbid anyone might ever even think of lighting up a cigarette or anything else in it. She's kept the cloth upholstery and dashboard covered, so the interior is as clean as her kitchen. CD and cassette player, but you wouldn't like her music. She's reluctantly agreed to part with it so that we can get a larger truck to pull the RV. Call me quick before she changes her mind again.

The truck sold in just two days. The response was overwhelming and I was able to rehome My Pretty Pony with another single gal who's driving her with the same kind of love I gave her. Brenda adopted her and took her to live in West Virginia, where, as far as I know, she still serves as a reliable workhorse. Her successor is a much more substantial Toyota Tundra that I have dubbed the Black Stallion. He leans into the hitch like a champ taking us over hill and dale and to places that were not accessible with the smaller vehicle. Parting with my first truck was my initial wrestling match with attachment in preparation for full-time travel. As it is for all who chose the mobile life, it would not be the last. We would soon need to examine our attachment to all our other worldly-goods and finally to our home itself.

Cutting the Career Cord

But in the interim, the second big attachment that I needed to deal with was to my job. In addition to the income, my career had been a source of identity and pride of accomplishment. It had given me security as a single person to live comfortably and the means to help my family when needed. I was grateful to work for a company with such good people and those daily relationships were important to me. Saying goodbye and shifting towards retirement wasn't an easy process. But I knew that if I delayed departure for too long, health would eventually become an obstacle to making significant life changes. Hesitating could mean that my dream of a life of travel could go unrealized. I did not want business and work to become my entire story and legacy.

I planned my departure out a full year in advance, giving myself and my company adequate time to choose a successor. I had time to implement training that supported my team and preserved the business relationships I had built. I drew up a plan and gradually faded back, allowing time to gear up and prepare concurrently for our traveling. If you are lucky enough to have a workplace that can accommodate your personal needs and timeline as you retire, I would recommend a gradual easing back. It is one good way to emotionally detach from this aspect of life.

You may be planning to permanently leave the season of life in which you have labored daily. Or, you may be planning on continuing to work from the road in some fashion. Either way, paring down can create some discomfort. At the same time, it creates space for other kinds of abundance. You must leave behind the role of a traditional job if you are to go off wandering. As you empty yourself, literally and figuratively, of all the trappings of a regular career, you will make room for a different kind of work in which you are a more active participant. A fresh and emptier state allows for the possibility of a broader and more expansive view of how and why you labor, one that is less conforming and often more satisfying. With fewer traditional trappings pressing down upon you, you can regroup in the community of people who have turned away from the season of life in which nine to five is so defining.

Cherished Treasures versus Excess Stuff

When you decide to RV full time, your perspective on possessions shifts out of necessity. I am not talking about a slight shift, but more of a cataclysmic movement in what we value. Commonly known as stuff or junk, we have accumulated collections of memorabilia and trinkets from years of long past adventures that have taken on mythical significance. Most of this stuff has no value other than the intrinsic value of good memories and it weighs us down heavily, impeding our goal to live mobile and with less.

Since Arnie and I fall somewhere between the ascetics who live minimally (me) and the hoarders who can part with nothing (Arnie), we were destined to face some challenges. Parting with some things was pretty easy and parting with others was almost unimaginable. I have moved my worldly goods many times over the years. Repeatedly I have carefully wrapped and unwrapped carved wooden birds painted by seventh-grade children in the Cayman Islands, colorful maracas from Venezuela and a huge ceremonial drum from China. Moving into a new home has never been complete until I have accomplished the ritual of placing treasured trinkets in a prominent place. My next new home, however, was going to be a comparatively tiny space calling for a significant purge.

The attachment to objects isn't always a bad thing. Cherished objects can be meaningful, comforting reminders of people and places and serve as bridges to other times in our lives. It may be making too light of the matter to quip that, "It's just stuff." or "It's only things." Some of those objects are symbolic vessels holding the meaning that we project upon them. Think about the Christian cross, which for devotees is a religious object that transcends being just a thing. The same thing holds true for a menorah or a statue of the Buddha. The comforting ritual of placing these objects in our personal spaces makes our environment soulful. Permanently parting with family treasures may trigger regret later on when you cease your nomadic life. You may once again wish to surround yourself with tender reminders of those people who loved us and those places we loved. These are the things that we value that we may need to consider taking with us or putting into storage for safekeeping. There may be hobbies that we will wish to resume at a later time. Keeping the antique motorcycle, the quilting machine, or the skiing equipment might make sense for some. Although storing Arnie's extensive baseball card collection might not have been practical, we still did it. We decided that the sentimental value of a hobby he has worked on since boyhood outweighed the cost of storage space.

We met a full-timing couple at a campground in Tennessee. Earl and Judy traveled in a large luxury motor coach and were there to attend a *Fly-In* [3], an event for remote model airplane enthusiasts. Earl shared a flyer for the event with us. We were initially a bit puzzled as to how he could participate in this event, given all of the equipment that would be needed to build and fly the models. With a bit of a sly grin, he waved us over to his tag-along utility trailer. "Look at what's hiding in here." When he dropped the tailgate, we were stunned to see a beautifully organized and fully stocked shop with all of his models and tools and equipment. These aren't tiny hobby shop model airplanes, but rather large replicas built by hand from plans, not kits. Earl's mobile hobby shop would be the envy of anyone who loved this sport. "It's taken me a couple of years to figure it all out, but now I have everything I need to work on the planes at my fingertips. I don't need a house with a large shop, just an organized space with all the right tools and supplies." Judy shared that she very much enjoys attending the Fly-Ins too since she's gotten to know many of the wives. "We plan day trips while the guys are flying their planes. That way we get to see what we girls are interested in without dragging our bored husbands along."

Earl and Judy usually stay about three weeks nearby each event visiting with other flying fans and working on their models together. Judy shared how much the company of women has come to mean to her. "I've gotten closer women friends now than when I was home. We enjoy a lot in common. We read books together, shop together, hike and go to the movies. We especially like to visit local parks and botanical gardens together. We keep very busy and we get to see the sites in good company. When someone has a medical issue, we know we have each other to count on. In between events, we all go our separate ways and then meet up at the next Fly-In. Happy hour is 4:00 each day and dinners are pot luck several times a week. It's a good life."

Earl and Judy are traveling with a purpose. They detached from everything but the items that were a priority for them. They made room for the equipment that they need to continue their favorite pastimes and still travel across the country doing it. In doing so, they have also crafted a wandering network of folks sharing the same interests, helping one another when needs arise.

Another couple that we enjoyed meeting was Rick and Sharon. They had one of the most pared-down situations that we have encountered. Rick and Sharon had wholly divested themselves of everything and had been traveling for nearly five years in a 32-foot Jayco bunkhouse with their two small parrots. The small bunk room had been adapted for the brightly colored birds' every comfort and was mainly a big birdcage. Toys dangled everywhere and perches were placed strategically so the small parrots could look out the window. It was a fully equipped bird playroom. Sharon shared that they are happy with their choice to travel full time for now. "We're not sure what the next step is, but for now, we're just winging it. No pun intended."

For some, it will not be necessary to downsize at all. We have several traveling friends who decided to keep their homes turnkey and fully furnished. They conveniently return home for holidays and family functions and then head back out on the road once again. It has worked best for them to maintain both their land-based home and their mobile home too. They have avoided downsizing- at least for the moment.

Sorting It All Out

However, most folks will need to downsize to some degree. The time finally came for us when we could not procrastinate any longer. We needed to get proactive about finding a proper home for all these treasures so as not to leave this legacy of junk to chance. First, we explained to the adult kids that the next generation must step into our shoes and receive the gift of stewardship of family things.

Passing along family treasures to the next generation was a common theme in interviews and the ambivalence that many folks have towards taking this step is apparent. Kids have their own style and taste and often do not want the burden of caring for family things that do not fit well into their homes. They likely do not have the same fondness and attachment for heirlooms and they are understandably not excited about these items that we have treasured for years. This can leave us feeling sad and rejected.

Our solution was to make it abundantly clear to the adult children and grandchildren that the decisions were theirs regarding what to do with the items we gifted to them. No gift comes with a superimposed guilt trip from us. We do not expect to see anything displayed in their more updated homes and we promise not to ask any questions. They could stuff it in a closet or pass it along to someone who could use it. In fact, we were so pleased to hear that some of the multiple sets of china were shared with family friends who loved vintage.

And so we passed down the old Irish doilies, the teacups, exquisite sets of china and precious handwritten cookbooks. Tiny baby blankets and outfits that babies came home from the hospital in were unearthed from the cedar chest and given to those grown children. First-grade artwork, letters to Santa, the Easter Bunny and the Tooth Fairy are now with their respective creators. We passed on the oak dining room table and hutch that my grandmother saved for so many years to buy. The first edition books that my grandfather read to me went to a grandson whose artistic soul will appreciate them.

After the kids received the family heirlooms that they probably didn't want, we turned to friends. The massage table went out the door to a friend who could use it, the colossal crockpot right behind it and the giant Lazy-Boy sofa has a new home with someone who liked it. A couple of yard sales rounded out the distribution. Letting go of all of the holiday decorations collected over so many years was hard, but the result is an unexpected feeling of lightness. We could breathe easier now. No longer would every weekend be spent cleaning, organizing, polishing and caring for a house and its contents. We were light-years closer to realizing our dream of wandering full-time.

As we disengaged from our belongings to hit the road, we also decided to disengage from some of the electronic attachments that take over our lives. When we are sitting at home with high-speed internet, it is easy to spend hours in front of the computer or on social media. It is tempting to park in the recliner watching an endless parade of celebrities and politicians on cable TV. On the road, we still have some access to all of this but are less inclined to binge away hours of our lives on sedentary pursuits. There is too much to discover, explore and learn about. We decided to keep the smartphone for navigating and the iPad for reading. The desktop was packed up and we switched over to a small laptop for email, bookkeeping and writing. We crafted a balance between the convenience of electronic devices and the freedom found when we made them an addition to our lifestyle and not its focus.

As you lighten up materially, you will make space both physically and mentally. You will free yourself to feel the seasons, the tides, the closing of each night and the rising of each day. You can fill your senses with the pure color of bluegrass in Kentucky and notice the way wisteria drapes gracefully off a tree in Georgia. It will be easier to smell the wild pine forest in Maine and more joyful to dip your hand in a frigid fast-flowing stream in Montana. You'll draw the primordial humidity of Big Cypress Swamp into your lungs. You can fully listen to the roar of the Mad River in New Hampshire as she rolls and churns over eons-old boulders telling you that you have all you need. These experiences fill our minds and hearts in a way that no possession can.

[1] https://medicine.yale.edu/news/yale-medicine-magazine/when-viewing-their-own-possessions-hoarders-brains-light.aspx

[2] https://www.napo.net/search/custom.asp?id=3767

[3] https://www.modelaircraft.org/event-calendar

Chapter Six
Rehearsal Dinner

"I warm up at home. I hit the stage. I'm ready,
whether it's rehearsal or anything."
- Louis Armstrong

Let's assume that you have gone through the process of examining all the pros and cons of living in an RV full-time. Let's move forward on the premise that you have decided that the roadie life is for you, or you are leaning strongly in that direction. If so, the *resfeber* has kept you under its spell. Resfeber is a fantastic Swedish word that really has no English equivalent. It refers to the restless race of the traveler's heart before the journey begins when anxiety and anticipation are tangled together. If you find yourself in a state of resfeber, I have one big piece of practical advice to offer. Try it out first before you put that For Sale sign in your front yard, or buy an RV and vamoose for parts unknown. There is a reason that rehearsal dinners are a tradition before the actual marriage ceremony; they increase the chances of getting it right.

This is not to say that you cannot be successful in this transition if you simply take the leap without pre-planning. Many travelers we have met did precisely that, survived the bumps and are still happily full-timing. However, if you have the chance to pre-plan and work into this new lifestyle slowly, you will encounter fewer obstacles and potential disappointments along the way.

Arnie and I practiced traveling for several years by taking extended vacations in a small hybrid RV that made an excellent starter unit. When we began spending half the year on the road we traded for a larger unit that made full-timing and hosting more comfortable. For this phase of our traveling, we chose a spacious Heartland Caliber that served us well while we contracted with the Army Corp of Engineers for three summers, returning to our Florida home in the winter. It was a gradual stepping up from shorter trips to half-time to full-time. This easing into full-timing gave us a chance to try the lifestyle on and ease into it at a practiced pace. Some variation of this might work for you, or you may just prefer to shorten the process to suit your situation. There is no one right way to make the move.

As you consider your transition, a degree of practice is prudent, even if it's just a maiden voyage of some sort. You might consider starting with a few shorter manageable trips to work the bugs out. Shakedown cruises are an opportunity to tweak your equipment and try out life on the road. A series of shorter trial run trips will give you a flavor of what it would be like to commit to full-time RVing. Trying on the RV lifestyle before you sell the house and divest yourself of all your worldly goods is just good common sense.

After all, for most of us, a house isn't just a house. The final decision to altogether leave my home and its memories in order to open the door to making new ones was a choice fraught with ambivalence. John O'Donohue, the Irish poet, author, priest and Hegelian scholar, writes lyrically about what our homes mean to us in this excerpt from Beauty:

> *"A home isn't simply a building; it is the shelter around the intimacy of a life. Coming in from the outside world and its rasp of force and usage, you relax and allow yourself to be who you are. The inner walls of a home are threaded with the textures of one's soul, a subtle weave of presences. If you could see your home through the lens of the soul, you would be surprised at the beauty concealed in the memory your home holds. When you enter some homes, you*

sense how the memories have seeped to the surface, infusing the aura
of the place and deepening the tone of its presence. Where love has
lived, a house still holds the warmth. Even the poorest home feels
like a nest if love and tenderness dwell there."

Eventually, I worked it through and came to a point in the thought process where I could see that supporting the RV and the now empty house made no practical sense. I eventually was able to achieve a proper perspective and in the end, entrust it graciously to another family. I do admit to a lump in my throat as I tucked the key under the doormat that one last time. Maybe a balance of part-time RVing and part-time living in your home will make sense to you also as a way to bridge the divide. You will need to decide what works best and whether you ease into the mobile lifestyle or just cut the cord and adopt it quickly. Some folks may never cut that cord but instead, keep their home base as well as traveling. There is no right or wrong way to enjoy living a nomadic life, be it full-time or part-time.

Arnie and I became part of the community of escapees from the corporate rat-race when we fully retired in 2015. Before that, we dabbled in travel part-time, making use of any vacation time to work the kinks out of our plan to be on the road. For many moons, we deliberated about the perfect time and place to leave our house behind for at least most of the calendar year. After a whirlwind year of turning 65, retiring and getting married, we were feeling the call of the open road and the need for a great adventure. We settled on getting our feet wet first by spending some extended time camping in the Great Smoky Mountains of Virginia and Tennessee. Here we could disengage and immerse ourselves in the beautiful natural landscape. In these awe-inspiring places, we could breathe and clear our minds from the clutter of so many years of stressful corporate jobs.

Cooking Up a Transition

We quickly realized that there was one particular area of our
mobile digs that would need a rehearsal dinner. We had to do
some severe cord-cutting in the kitchen. What we did not realize
until later was that focusing on the kitchen was not only teaching
us about downsizing into RV living, it was also helping us to
learn about connecting with others on the road.

We decided to concentrate on the kitchen first because, for us,
this room is symbolic. We are foodies who love to cook and the
kitchen has always been the epicenter of our home. It is the
space where everything good for the body and soul takes place
and it holds great significance and meaning for us. It is where
family and friends have come together over and over in love.
Taking apart the kitchen would be a real test of how serious we
were about getting ourselves to the point where we could move
into an RV full-time. If we could do it in the kitchen, we could
do it in all the other areas that would require downsizing.

At the time that we launched our adventures, we owned a tiny
hybrid Jayco Featherlite that we fondly dubbed *Dinky Doo*. It had
a very compact living space and both ends folded out into
canvas enclosed double beds. As a starter unit Dinky Doo served
us perfectly for long camping weekends and we made some great
memories with her in tow. But now we were considering longer
periods on the road and we were not sure how we could store
kitchen equipment and adequate staples in Dinky. With plans to
travel to some remote locales when supplies were not readily
available, we strategized about storage containers and kitchen
cabinet organizers. A friend lent us a shrink wrap gadget to por-
tion out compact packets of grains, beans, nuts, popcorn and
granola that stored easily. We were beginning to look like
survivalists planning for the zombie apocalypse.

A Cooking Reduction

Some kitchen gadgets were harder to part with than others. I gazed lovingly at the big green Margarita Machine as if it were a beloved aging Pekingese, dreading the day that I would need to part with it. I took it on a few trial runs and then decided that it just took up too much space. If I wanted a Margarita, I would find a good bar rather than devote half of my kitchen counter space to the footprint this mammoth required. Thank goodness for our friends who were willing to give it a good home and promised that we could visit and enjoy it anytime. We quickly learned that we took too much other equipment also. Through trial and error, we figured out how to reduce down to a few essentials that can do double duty in an RV kitchen.

Nowadays, the trailer kitchen is much lighter. Arnie makes his morning coffee in a french press and the bulky twelve cup coffee maker is a thing of the past. The Pampered Chef potato masher, a treasured gift from my fellow wandering pal Carol, also makes an excellent whip or slotted spoon. The electric skillet can sauté, fry and even boil spaghetti, replacing the need for various size pans. A versatile induction plate replaces the open flame of the gas stove and because I don't use the gas stove often, its' closed top does double duty as more counter space. Tupperware bowls do triple duty serving as storage, mixing bowls and serving dishes as needed. Mugs that are freezer, oven and microwave safe accommodate morning coffee, soup, pudding, ice cream and also store leftovers in the fridge. We keep pans and dishes all nested like a set of Russian dolls, each fitting into the next to save space. Every piece that we take along is examined for redundancy and thoughtfully removed or allowed to remain on board. It's incredible what you can do without and still whip up a gourmet meal or simple, hearty fare in a tiny space using a few key pieces. With thoughtful planning and a few false starts, we are now able to prepare most anything we want and enjoy meals for just the two of us or cook for a crowd.

Paring Down

The cookbook collection was next on the list. We knew there was no way we were going to be able to travel with our extensive collection of much-loved cookbooks, but dismantling it was a bit like slicing into my soul. The weight alone would be prohibitive and it made no sense to give up the amount of space they would require. At the same time, each of them contained favorite recipes that we enjoyed. Our solution was to compile a pared-down collection of tried and true recipes that we can easily put together in a small space kitchen with the equipment we keep on board. Each favorite was copied and put into a lightweight three-ring binder that fits nicely into a nook in an overhead cabinet. All recipes took into consideration the cost and availability of ingredients, as well as the space needed to store them. All of the ingredients in these recipes are also flexible enough to capitalize on local finds. Making this space-saving and personalized recipe book was an enjoyable project that helped us to think spatially about what we could take with us. We would later replicate the model with a binder for important papers, one for maps and routes and another for healthcare records.

Cutting the cord on our much-loved collection of cookbooks had a hidden benefit that we did not expect. It inadvertently helped us meet a personal goal; to be mindful of what we eat and make socially conscious food choices. For the RV cookbook, we methodically organized recipes and meal plans that were healthy and mostly vegetarian and then we conducted rehearsal dinners to make sure we had included the meals we enjoy the most. The collection of recipes for camping provided a blueprint to utilize ingredients that were as farm to table and fair trade as possible, one of our original goals on the dream wall. With tried and true recipes at our fingertips and without storing ingredients that don't fit into our new lifestyle, we have the room to more easily incorporate fresh fruits and vegetables, local cheeses and wines into our menus when there is access to them.

To meet our goal of buying and eating local foods, we frequently stop for available sources of local produce. Fruits and veggies are high on the list of what we like to eat, but in our small space there was precious little storage room. Ditching the habit of buying in bulk to buy more frequently and in smaller quantities was an adjustment. If there are no farms, farmers markets or other local sources within reasonable driving distance from our route, we ask a "local" to please direct us to some hidden gem. It was in just this manner that we discovered Mayhaw jelly from Georgia and it is now one of our very favorite treats, available seasonally from folks who sell it out in front of their homes at roadside stands. It is fun to try regional produce that is not readily available at home and we enjoy working new products into our menu. We watch for church bake sales where we can get homemade bread and an occasional sweet treat. When we happen upon church suppers, we enjoy stopping in as they are our very favorite way to enjoy a meal with others. You can do a quick internet search to see if there are any nearby where you're staying. It's an excellent way to get a feel of the local area and they invariably offer a friendly welcome to all. Take your Tupperware and purchase an extra meal for the next day on the road.

One foodie encounter stands out as memorable. Driving along a dusty back road in central Georgia, Arnie and I stopped at one of the many roadside stands selling fresh vegetables and peaches from the field. There was a large handmade red and black sign announcing the much anticipated Vidalia onion season. [1] This delicious variety of sweet onion grows only in a specific region of Georgia. They are seasonal, so we try to enjoy the moment

71

and use them in as many recipes as possible while we have access to them.

Learning from Chance Encounter

On this particular day, we pulled over and exited our air-conditioned truck into an oven blast of hot, humid air. We stepped over the fat black lab snoring on the pathway leading up to the produce stand. He was oblivious to everything around him. Our sneakers crunched across the red Georgia clay as we approached the counter where we saw the onions packaged in quantities far greater than we could store or use. "Do you sell any loose onions? We're traveling in that trailer over there and can only handle smaller amounts of perishables at a time."

The affable old fellow behind the counter looked like a Shar-Pei-one of those wrinkled dogs. He must have spent a lifetime of hours in the Vidalia fields under the Georgia sun to earn those stripes. "You really need to get a whole bag."

Arnie took a crack at it. "A whole bag is a lot for just-"

The old man interrupted with a chuckle. "I'm going to tell you how to keep them. I'll bet you don't know."

I drew in a breath of the steamy heat and grinned back at him. "Okay, I'm game. Tell me how." I couldn't wait to unfold this conversation with him. He reached out a field-roughened hand. "My name is Eustace."

Eustace was a consummate salesman. "It's a secret, but I'll tell you how to keep them Vidalias for months past season's end." Eustace was very short, a little bent over and looked like he carried the wisdom of the world in his oversized overall pockets. He had that farmer's way about him that characterizes those who are in tune with what the earth gives and how to use it well. "When you knows this secret, you can buy a whole bag."

It was a day that would wilt a river, but Eustace was not one to hurry a story. "Do y'all cook 'em or eat 'em raw?" I shared that we often cut them up in salads or made French Onion soup since they're so sweet. He cocked a bushy gray eyebrow and stared at me as if I had just dropped from the sky.

"I juss bites em like an apple."

A few words and Eustace put Julia Child in her proper place. His eyes sparkled and his face crinkled even more. He was silently laughing at me about the onion soup.

"Here's what y'all do."

His instructions began in a slow sweet Georgia drawl. "You see them fancy long pants y'all got on? You take and cut one leg off real high. Y'all don't need to be wearing those hot things in this weather no how." Obviously, Eustace has never ridden on a long trip with Arnie with the AC set to frigid. That's the reason for long pants on a blistering Georgia day.

"After you cut that leg off, you get one of them plastic tie-offs and you tie off the bottom of the leg. Then you drop in an onion. Then you make another tie off and you drop in another onion. Then you tie it off again. Take another onion and you drop in that one. Just keep doin' that over and over. It keeps them from gassing off each other. That's what makes them turn bad. Like too many people in too small a space. They don't like being crowded. Understand now, Missy? Y'all want a five-pound bag or a ten-pound bag?"

Sweat running down his forehead and eager to get back in the cool truck, Arnie was sold. "We'll take that one. Ten pounds should fill up those pants my wife has on." With full intentions of putting Eustace's folksy advice to use when we got home, we climbed back into the truck and cranked the AC back to high. It cooled the truck right down and mitigated the overwhelming odor of ten pounds of onions in the back seat.

For dinner that night we had a delicious onion soup with a crouton and melted cheese in homage to a wise man on the side of the road who shared a bit of rural wisdom with us. Arnie asked me what was for dessert. Thanks to Eustace, we had plenty of onions, so I advised, "Just bite one like an apple."

Sharing Tastes

Meeting the people who grow our food has been a joy and, at times, an eye-opening experience. The stories of their callings are profound and enlightening. Occasionally, we have stepped far outside of our comfort zone with new food encounters and ended up crossing that particular item off our grocery list forever. Some regional foods take local instruction to prepare and appreciate them: i.e., southern country ham. Who knew it had to be soaked to remove the salt? We never had a rehearsal dinner for southern country ham and so, we ended up eating cold cereal that night.

We are interested in learning more about the network of people who are committed to ethical food production. Traveling gives us an exciting opportunity to learn firsthand about such small producers. And so, in South Carolina we've eaten field peas picked that very same morning, in Virginia, we enjoyed farm eggs laid in cage-free environments and freshly picked strawberries from the side of the road in North Carolina. We were the fortunate recipients of a loaf of fantastic bread baked by Mennonite hands. We spread the thick slabs with Mayhaw jelly and stirred honey from Alabama bees into our tea. It was fun to sample artisan goat cheese in Texas, but we passed on the curried goat hoagies. Using the resource, Local Harvest [2], you can locate wineries, farms and growers along your route. Check this out because with this membership you can boondock at no charge for the night while you visit their facility and enjoy their products.

Sometimes we pair up with other travelers that we meet and head out to a local spot for a meal or put together an impromptu potluck of our local finds. We found a new vision of what constitutes mobile community beginning to emerge as we opened ourselves to reaching out along the route and sharing a meal and a fire with fellow travelers. Setting a goal of experiencing local food helped us directly engage with our new mobile group and begin to integrate into it. As a bonus, we have learned much about the joys and challenges of feeding ourselves, our families and our nation.

James Beard said, "Food is maybe the only universal thing that really has the power to bring everyone together. No matter what culture, everywhere around the world people get together to eat." Arnie and I put so much thought into our mobile kitchen because we believe that what we create in that kitchen connects us with those who share our table and our fire. Although we all cook in different ways, food enables us to come together and speak a common language. With that common language, we come to the table for meaningful discussions. Sharing food transcends race, ethnicity, culture, age, sexuality and class as it calls us into community. When we carry our plates to sit around a shared fire, we comfort ourselves and one another.

[1] https://www.vidaliaonion.org/

[2] https://www.localharvest.org/

Chapter Seven
Wandering Mindfully

"In the beginner's mind, there are many possibilities, but in the expert's there are few."
- Shunryu Suzuki

In his classic book on the practice of Zen, the late Shunryu Suzuki [1] cautioned readers to avoid getting wrapped up in what you're doing so that you don't miss the point entirely. Old-timers would say, "Don't miss the forest for the trees." On many levels, this is valuable advice for us nomads. Arnie and I do our best to nurture an awareness of what is around us and within us at any present moment. Being mindful is a tall order somedays.

I found myself at risk of missing the forest for the trees in our second summer of camp hosting in Massachusetts at a gorgeous Army Corps of Engineers project location where our campsite was set in a quarter-acre clearing with a dense pine woods surrounding the campsite. The site was a perfect natural setting with room for raised bed gardens, turkeys wandering through the clearing, owls hooting at night and a roomy space for the dogs to romp. This summer host site was a bird watchers paradise and we had a constant crook in our necks from looking up with binoculars to see what species were calling from the trees. The project manager had built us a great fire pit for sharing campfires. It was a joy to sit around it with visiting family and friends after they enjoyed a swim in the old fashioned swimming hole, Harrisons Beach. Camp hosts couldn't ask for a more beautiful natural setting at which to spend a New England summer.

We'd decided to accept this particular host job placement because it would allow us to spend time with our new grandson, Nolan. What an immeasurable gift it was to welcome him into the family and bond with our first grandchild together. We loved going to visit him on our days off. We loved everything about this little guy. We loved the way he smelled, the way he cooed and even the way he threw up all over his grandpa every time Arnie picked him up. New baby Nolan made everything worthwhile that summer.

Facing Inconveniences

But there are compromises to make when you become a cord cutter and move your full-time residence into an RV. At this beautiful location, there was no reliable Wi-Fi and no cable TV. Cell service was spotty and maybe most disappointing, there was no washer and dryer. Paying bills, keeping up with the news, making essential calls and doing laundry meant a trip into town. On one of my days off, when there was a lot to accomplish, the inconveniences were getting on my last raw nerve. And so was Arnie. He was practicing his gift of being able to relax with a cup of coffee while all of the day's tasks stare him right in the face. I on the other hand, feel the weight of household responsibilities more urgently. I needed to do some bookkeeping that required Wi-Fi, I wanted to make calls to check in with family and the odiferous laundry was overflowing the bedroom. In addition, we were out of DVD's to watch.

"I can feel a meltdown coming on. I'm going down to the water and meditate to get some perspective. I'm trying to remember why we're here and what we were thinking. This is all so much work." Arnie agreed that it would be a sage idea for me to go somewhere and get a grip.

I marched down to the beach, plunked down in the sand and began my meditation routine. It wasn't very long before I heard the resident family of ducks calling across the pond and mother phoebe from her nest in the woods behind me. A cool breeze rippled across the pond carrying the scent of cedar trees and it arrived soft and welcome against my skin. The sand was warming in the morning sun and cradled me where I sat. My breathing relaxed and I began to examine the story I was telling myself.

In the pond side stillness, gradually the frustrations of RV life began to take on their proper size relative to everything. I was able to concede that I really could manage the absence of Wi-Fi at camp quite well. I had a summer resident pass to the Uxbridge Public Library, a friendly and welcoming place. Zach, the librarian, would see me coming and kindly turn the AC down so that I'd be comfortable to work. He would offer a bottle of water if I stayed there writing for a few hours. They have a terrific selection of DVD's and shelves full of new books, so who needs cable TV? I loved visiting this homey building with its oiled hardwood floors and carved woodwork; it was my summer haven and retreat. I appreciated being able to spend time writing there while soaking up the New England feel of this historic building's architecture. On the drive into the library, I could stop by a quintessential New England establishment and pick up a Dunkin. I could then use their Wi-Fi to pay a few bills and make calls to family to catch up. It's not so bad.

But then there is still the damn laundry. I'd have to meditate on that a while longer to get that smelly problem in perspective. Considering the money I've spent on laundromats, we probably could have purchased a rig that came fully equipped with a washer and dryer. The countless hours in run-down laundry facilities dodging cranky toddlers and college students on cell phones sometimes seem like a mindless life wasting exercise in patience.

Camping, by its very nature, generates laundry. The laundry basket is a witch's brew of jeans covered with stinky bug repellent, damp towels and sweaty summer socks that demands a weekly trip into town to the laundromat. Loading up sheets, blankets and baskets into the truck and then huffing them into the busy laundry isn't my idea of fun. It's a regular timeline of Tide, Febreeze and quarters to feed the machines. And the funny thing about laundry is that no matter how often you do it, it's never done. There is no end and apparently no beginning to the process of laundering clothes. Laundry is a constant mundane flow.

But isn't it a fact that most circumstances and events in our lives are just that: a constant and mundane flow. Our lives too are a process of sorting tasks and activities into manageable loads. This white sock goes here and that navy towel goes there. The small decisions made while processing laundry aren't much different than the big decisions that impact our lives in bigger ways.

You could liken doing the laundry to how we'll take the soiled aspects of our lives, sort them out and clean them so that we have enough balance to be free to enjoy our RVing life. Sometimes it's just necessary to slow down, meditate and remember why we decided to cut the cord in the first place.

Joseph Campbell said, "You must give up the life you planned in order to have the life that's waiting for you." It's normal to feel a bit purposeless at times when we leave behind the chores associated with living in a house to move into an RV, especially at the beginning of our travels. We don't need to mow the lawn, clean the gutters, or plant the flower beds anymore. It's no longer necessary to walk to the mailbox, dust the living room, or stack the woodpile. Many people find comfort in the rhythmic ritual and grounding routine of everyday life. Without rituals and routines, some folks can begin to feel adrift. Some wanderers come to a place in their journey where they needed to find some structure. They feel the need for a rudder for a while rather than just drifting from place to place.

Hosting: Wandering with a Tether

There were times when I began to feel like I'd taken on wandering with no end in sight and that I was anchorless. Some days it was hard to call up the game plan and find the rule book for free-falling. Intellectually I knew that we had goals and a mission for our travel, but sometimes I just missed having a bit of structure to balance out the movement. I have to admit that after a period of being without a home base, I was feeling untethered and it was honestly a bit unnerving at times. Park hosting came along at just the right time.

Park hosting for the Army Corps was a perfect antidote for us when we started to feel an itch for more structure to our wandering. It offered a blend of being in a fixed location for a few months and then returning to the road for the rest of the year. By pausing the journey, we were able to infuse the traveling with a more mindful routine that was refreshing and renewing. Staying the summer gave us lots of time to get to know the local area. We enjoyed listening to inspiring folk music and immersing ourselves in the history and culture of the Blackstone Valley. It was a blend of moving about and then settling for a few months with purpose and we found that to be a perfect balance for us. You'll discover and establish your comfortable balance between necessary motion and mindful pause as you embark on your journeys.

Developing Routines with a Purpose

Our first summer as hosts with the Army Corps allowed ample opportunity to work on my mindfulness practice. Meditating in the quiet forest of Massachusetts, I realized part of my frustration was not the inconveniences as much as the lack of daily structure or routine I had been accustomed to.

Hosting gave me a new set of routines. Early morning chores included sweeping the sand from the change house. As daybreak crept up over the shoreline, I swept out the building, moving the very same grains of sand that I'd swept outside yesterday. The rhythm of the broom scratching on the cement was a perfect accompaniment to mindful prayers. I love the sound of the old straw broom as it coaxed the pile outside once again. A broom is a tool of such elegant simplicity. It's satisfying to make that floor all clean and ready for the bare feet of dozens of children donning their bathing suits to go for a dip in the river. Even knowing that the sand would travel back inside the building by the end of the day couldn't diminish the satisfaction of performing this simple task mindfully.

When you elevate a repetitive task to the level of something Zen-like, you reintroduce purpose into the whole process. Sweeping the floor is something calming and meditative when you take the time to imagine the recipients of your efforts. I was able to transform a mundane task into a purposeful act when I reframed how I thought about sweeping with that broom. I could now think of it as a kindness done in preparation for a small child's play or a compassionate act that enabled an older person to sit and enjoy nature in a clean place.

I never looked at any housekeeping task with such insight when I was living in a large home. Most days, housework vexed me. It felt like I was just house cleaning myself into obscurity. Paradoxically, by cutting the cord on a large home to move into a RV, you may find that you've created the space to think in more meaningful and mindful ways about the necessary routines of daily living.

Remaining Newbies

As the Massachusetts summers came to a close, it was time to hit the road again. We would return to host at this same park for several years. And as time went on and we became more accustomed to moving about, we found that we had to plan less intensively. We were moving into a more mature phase of our traveling life. We now would challenge ourselves to balance all of the planning with a commitment to wing it more. We'd start to experiment with being more spontaneous and not worry quite so much about the "what-ifs," or the "might happens."

Without really knowing when it happened, we'd accepted the fact that we would always be beginners. We're continuous learners who don't need to have an expert grasp on all aspects of RVing to have a successful nomadic experience. While some preparation is undoubtedly a prudent practice for the transition to RVing, we began to understand that we didn't need to plan every single detail. We were at a stage in our travels where we'd adopted a more laisse fair attitude, staying open to chance encounters. We thought of ourselves as being students of the experience as we go along. We'd realized that this new life is a process of adjustment and it is okay to make changes to the original plan as you go along.

Cutting the literal and figurative cords to the past liberates our minds to be ready for the present journey. If your mind is empty of past attachments, it's always available for new experiences. By adopting a beginner's mind, you can learn to travel with more attention to where you are right now, free from bias, views and opinions that prevent us from listening more deeply to the people we encounter as we wander.

Moving On

The aching homesickness for the familiar people, places and things from our Florida home resolved as we moved deeper into our community of other wanderers. If we never arrived anywhere, it didn't matter now. I felt the past becoming muted and the present coming into clear focus. Along the way, living in the RV had shifted me. I now could appreciate a small patch of yellow sunlight traveling across green grass towards a New England pond as much as a week of perfect sunny days in my Florida home. And I was happy with the shift.

In Arkansas, we met a woman who is one of many solevagants, people who make their journey alone. Rebecca is a slight woman in her mid-thirties with soft curly short hair who travels with a goofy Great Dane twice her size. She and Boomer have an understanding and this gentle giant respects her space when they walk, moving cautiously to avoid bumping into her. Rebecca has the early stages of MS and at times, leans on him for stability. She doesn't appear built for the rough and tumble of traveling alone, but she's much tougher than her first impression. She and I shared a campfire well into one dark night and I enjoyed hearing about her courageous journey, the literal one and the spiritual one.

"I lost a baby in my late twenties and my marriage never recovered from it. Looking back, I'm sure there were other issues, but when my pregnancy ended unexpectedly, it was the straw that broke the camel's back. My husband and I divorced soon after that." She continued matter-of-factly telling me her story as we watched the tendrils of the fire flicker upward.

"My friends didn't seem to know what to say or how to help. They just drifted away and I didn't hear from them for weeks or months, or maybe I pushed them away. Who knows? But my lost baby moved in to stay and I couldn't figure out how to move on and live a normal life again. In my whole life, I had never been alone. I had gone from my parents' home to college and right on to marriage, surrounded by my husbands' large Italian family. I didn't have the slightest clue of how to be alone with myself. I always looked at other people to solve my dilemmas. I went to work for a large tech firm and was on a rising career path. I couldn't be still - ever. After the divorce, I was alone for the first time in my life and I was surprised to find how much I liked it. Mostly I liked it because I could drink myself into oblivion and no one would know or get on my case about it. I was so lost." We sat in silence for a few moments and I looked quietly into the comfort of the fire, waiting for her to continue with her story.

"The longer I was alone, the more I craved the quiet and the independence. One night I watched a program on PBS by Ken Burns about the national parks [2]. I got the crazy notion that I wanted to travel and see every one of those parks. It struck me like a thunderbolt. I could find what was missing if I went actively looking for it. I didn't relish the idea of spending so much intense time with another person. I decided to go solo. I also knew that I couldn't drive drunk across the country, so I quit drinking cold turkey. I sobered up, did some route planning and took off alone in my van with my dog for company and here I am. My family thought I had the sense that God gave geese to undertake this by myself, but for once, I held my ground and stood by my own decision."

Rebecca shared that in addition to Ken Burns, she was inspired by Exodus 14:14: *"The Lord will fight for you; you need only be still."* She'd been traveling for over a year solo, still working for the same tech company remotely as a consultant. Rebecca no longer had the stress of going to an office and keeping a nine-to-five schedule. "I'm healthy, happy and have patience with myself and with the curveballs this life throws me. RVing has taught me how to quiet down my busy brain and I do better work because of it."

Rebecca has developed a network of other women who are traveling solo and they meet up for fellowship and support at times. "I never valued my women friends as much as I should have and I never knew what a community of sisters was out there. I joined RVing Women [3], so even though I travel solo, I never feel alone. Before I started traveling and meeting such strong independent women, I viewed other women as being in a sort of competition with me. When I divorced, I discovered that there is a whole sisterhood that's interested in growing and discovering themselves as women together. I don't feel any pressure to achieve or attain anymore. I never expected the kindness I found from other women who travel. The collective experience is invaluable to me as a solo and I rely on my women friends for advice and direction when I run into problems on the road. I hope I help them too in return."

<u>Finding Peace</u>

Rebecca shared that she has a sense of peace now with her loss. "I still mourn the loss of my baby acutely at times. But she's along for the ride with me. I talk to my daughter and tell her about all of the places Boomer and I are seeing and I remind her that she's a part of them. If God is everywhere and in all things, then my little girl is also with me wherever I go. If I wake up to a day that's not easy, I often reach out to my RVing Women friends. I go slower, more mindfully and try to be more patient with myself just as I'd be to my child if she were here traveling with us. That's how I get through it all. One day at a time, as they say."

Rebecca had found she belongs with a new group of women who, like herself, were crafting their lives with mindfulness. All who wander aren't lost; Rebecca was indeed no longer lost. Is developing stillness and patience with ourselves one path to happiness? Perhaps Rebecca had discovered a key. Every day she gives herself the precious gift of time to be mindful of the experience she's having. As the miles rolled beneath our wheels, Arnie and I are often still with one another for many miles. We seem content with the view out the window and the voyage of self-discovery we're on together. We don't seem to need the radio on as much or the music playing in the background. We pause in the journey more frequently to get out and explore.

Wandering has freed us to halt along the way and dissolve ourselves into the landscape. We have practiced sitting mindfully in grassy fields, under groves of pine trees, on the side of cotton fields and along rock formations. Practicing stillness has helped us both to become more present and less attached. We are better able to transcend the cares of the past. With each new travel day, we're beginners again, awakening with the awareness that the earth gives us sacred space. This sacred space allows peacefulness to come as naturally as sleep if we but stop and sit still with it awhile.

[1] https://www.dailyzen.com/journal/zen-mind-beginners-mind

[2] http://www.pbs.org/nationalparks/

[3] https://www.rvingwomen.org/

Chapter Eight
Choice or Necessity?

"Nothing is more active than thought for it travels over the universe, and nothing is stronger than necessity for all must submit to it."
- Thales

When I first began thinking about traveling full-time, I perceived the contemporary nomadic lifestyle to be a choice. Driving to work on the interstate, I would glance longingly at the pickup trucks pulling sleek fifth wheels and wonder where they might be heading. I envied their seemingly carefree existence, free of responsibility and the drudgery of the commute. At that point in the process, I saw only the surface and I didn't fully understand that each one had a unique story about reducing complicated lives built up over many years to the size of an RV.

Later, when I began interviews with those who are doing it, they quickly enlightened me that this isn't always the case. Sometimes, RV living is a necessity, not a choice. I heard many stories from people of all ages that revealed poignant circumstances calling courage and stamina along with a new lifestyle. Each story is different.

Reimagining Retirement

Many members of the baby boomer generation were in the late stages of preparing for retirement when they found themselves caught in this series of complex events that contributed to the bad economy at that time. Many chose to walk away from homes that would never in their lifetimes represent suitable investments for them. They worked all of their lives to pay off their homes before retirement and their equity was gone. A percentage of them are now full-timers and they have crafted a new lifestyle, albeit it an unanticipated one. Many of them are couples, but there are a significant number of both men and women who travel solo.

We have encountered scores of travelers who have no home base due to devastating financial losses during the housing bubble when they lost their homes to foreclosure. Many factors came into play during that time that caused good people to fall prey to mortgage fraud schemes. These schemes crashed down around American homeowners, decimating their retirement savings and changing their lives forever. [1] Folks who worked all their lives in anticipation of a comfortable retirement have had to wholly reimagine the circumstances of their later years.

In these situations, it is generally not a choice at all but rather, a living arrangement that is the only affordable alternative available. These folks are not technically homeless, but they are "houseless," living in RVs, trailers and vans while driving from one seasonal location to another to pick up jobs. Many of the positions are low-wage and offer little or no benefits. People in this situation are downwardly mobile older American citizens and to call their living arrangement a "recreational" vehicle is deceiving. Theirs is not a life of recreation, but rather, a life of necessity. And, because it is so difficult to save enough money to move up and out of their nomadic life, they are easily exploited by employers who do not provide ideal conditions for itinerant workers.

Jessica Bruder [2] teaches at the Columbia School of Journalism and is an award-winning journalist whose work focuses on subcultures and the darker corners of the American economy. Her book, *Nomadland, Surviving America in the Twenty-First Century*, takes a disturbing look at the lives of transient older adults who make up this low-cost labor pool. Her story is a revelation that may provide a hint of what is to come as the U.S. population of older adults who have survived the Great Recession continue to age on the road. It is also a tale of a demographic of resilient and creative people who persevere through misfortune and financial hardship to make a new life outside of what we consider ordinary roots.

> *"There have always been itinerants, drifters, hobos, restless souls. But now, in the second millennium, a new kind of wandering bribe is emerging. People who never imagined being nomads are hitting the road. They're giving up traditional houses and apartments to live in what some call "wheelestate"- vans, secondhand RVs, schoolbuses, pickup trucks, travel trailers and plain old sedans. They are driving away from the impossible choices that face what used to be the middle class. Decisions like: Would you rather have food or dental work? Pay your mortgage or your electric bill? Make a car payment or buy medicine? Cover rent or student loans? Purchase warm clothes or gas for your commute? For many, the answer seemed radical at first. You can't give yourself a raise, but what about cutting your biggest expense? Trading a stick-and-brick domicile for life on wheels?"*
>
> *- Jessica Bruder, Nomandland: Surviving America in the Twenty-First Century*

Families on the road

During my interviews, I anecdotally found that the families I talked with fell into two distinct groups.

For the first group, living in an RV isn't an adventure for them; it's a necessity. We most often encountered this situation in campgrounds where there are non-transient sites available. These campgrounds cater to people who plan to stay longer or even indefinitely. In these situations, the children attend the local public school and take advantage of local resources. Sometimes the families were more truly itinerant, working from the road in

91

seasonal jobs. Here is the issue though- while each story varied when I talked with them, usually the family told of some crisis that caused them to lose housing. All of the stories told to me in interviews by families in this situation were without exception, heartbreaking.

The second group of families is having quite a different experience. These are families that are traveling by choice and making the parks their classroom. They conceptualize their travels as an adventure and are homeschooling their children. They most often still claim state residence and have a fixed mailing address with family or with one of the mail services available to RVers. Their plans are generally time-limited and they expect to go back to traditional living situations after a set amount of time.

A Family Traveling by Necessity

In a modest West Virginia state campground, I sat down with Christine, a grandmother in her late sixties who travels with her husband and nine-year-old grandson. Christine is tall and lean, with her graying hair pulled back neat and tight in two long braids. She has a warm smile and a no-nonsense style about her. We met for an interview on the front porch of the cabin provided to her and her husband Royal while they serve as hosts. She said she's enjoying having the temporary extra space in addition to her trailer. "It gives me some extra room to get meals and to get away from the boys. We mostly do pretty well to-gether, but it's close quarters on rainy days for sure."

Christine and her husband had been serving as hosts at this campground all summer. Just prior, they'd worked at the golf club up the road and at the end of the season, they would leave for Florida to work in a state park for the winter. They have their work placements planned out ahead for a year to secure a place that's consistent with schooling for their grandson, Dakota.

Christine and I settled into a comfortable and familiar conversation about hosting, sharing notes and chuckling back and forth about some of the funny things that happen when you work with the public. We exchanged stories while relaxing in a front porch rocker with a beer and got to know one another a bit, realizing that we had been to many of the same locations and campgrounds. After a while, she shared how they came to be in their present circumstances. It wasn't by choice.

"West Virginia has a nasty drug problem and most families have a family member who's impacted by it in some way. Ours is no exception. It would be easy to look at my husband and me and think that we always had nothing and that traveling around cleaning bathrooms and campsites is what we've always done. But that's not how it is. Our daughter done us wrong. We helped her for years to try to get clean from meth and we finally just run out of money and declared bankruptcy. We lost our nice home and all our retirement money was gone to rehab for her. What we've got left is this trailer, each other and our grandson. I don't even know where my daughter is now. She's our only child and we never imagined life would be like this. Now we're raising a kid in our old age."

In the end, Christine and her husband lost their home base and their root community. They now travel from park to park hosting in exchange for hookups. They're living on Social Security and whatever odd jobs they can pick up. They have legal custody of their nine-year-old grandson who travels with them and they try to schedule their hosting placements around his needs as best they can. "We've got to take care of Dakota first. Ain't none of this his fault. He was three when he came to live with us and he don't know any other life than this one."

The bus dropped him off at the park as we talked and Dakota came charging up the road grinning from ear to ear. "Gramma, look at the picture of our house I did for you." It was a picture of their trailer that he'd colored in school.

Christine and her family belong to a population of families who are living in RVs out of necessity. There are more people in this position than is readily apparent since most move around and fly under the radar of officials. The debate about whether or not these families are indeed homeless is taking place in some homelessness advocacy circles. [3] Regardless, Dakota is a great kid. He's widely traveled and knows that his success is a priority for his grandparents. While it's not a traditional life for him at nine years old, it's still a rich one. Dakota's had diverse natural experiences that many kids who have much more than he does will never get to experience. At nine, Dakota can confidently read a road map and point out in the atlas all of the places where they have been. He enthusiastically told me that his favorite animal that he ever saw was a mountain goat in Idaho and then corrected that.

"No, wait a minute. I think it was a crocodile in Florida in the Everglades, right Gramma?" In spite of the poignant compromises to their retirement, Christine and Royal are doing a great job raising their grandson. And they're not alone. According to the same Association for Community Living report, approximately 1 million grandparents age 60 and over were responsible for the basic needs of one or more grandchildren under age 18 living with them in 2016. With the expansion of the growing wide-spread drug epidemic, this number can only increase.

Sonder is the French travel concept that every passer-by is living a life as vivid and complex as our own. Arnie and I stopped by Christine's campsite as we were driving out. We dropped off a new backpack, filled with school supplies for Dakota. Our thoughts still drift back to this little boy and we hope that he and his dedicated grandparents are thriving and doing well. [4]

A Family Traveling by Choice

We met one extraordinary young family who represented a group of committed and enlightened parents who homeschool from the road. We had a chance to share a few lively conversations over campfires with them during the week that we camped side by side. John and his wife May are the parents of six kids. They're homeschooling their family from a renovated 1989 coach that fairly rocks with activity. I have to admit that I groaned out loud when they pulled in beside us at one of our favorite rural bird-watching spots. I looked at Arnie as, one after another, the kids piled out, eager to inspect their new campsite. He rolled his eyes. "It doesn't appear that we'll be enjoying any peace and quiet for a while."

What we got in exchange for the compromised peace and quiet was well worth the trade-off. It was a privilege to get the chance to meet this family and see them in action. And I do mean in action. John and May are hands-on natural teachers who never miss a moment to instruct and enlighten their brood in such a gentle way. They both left their traditional academic jobs to set aside two years dedicated to giving their kids an alternative kind of educational experience. They were about eight months into their timeline when we met them. John talked about their commitment to teaching their children that they don't need to fit into an intellectual or spiritual box. "I want my kids to be known by what they're aligned with and not what they're against. We're teaching them that they don't have to choose between science and religion. Nor do they need to choose between their intellectual integrity and an imposed vision of faith." John wants to create for his young children- "a classroom in nature that encourages them to ask critical questions and speak their truths."

John and his wife believe that their mobile lifestyle will expose the children to opportunities to live in "real-time." He talked at length about how dedicated he and May are to making sure that their kids are aware of and involved in important issues. "We're visiting places that spark learning about racial reconciliation, social justice, religious diversity, good stewardship of the environment and spirituality. He said they're not looking to provide the kids with "simple answers but rather bring them to an unpretentious classroom that engages their whole hearts and minds." This family has a distinct purpose for their travel and they have done their homework to execute that purpose well. They belong to a tight-knit traveling network of other home-schooling families called Fulltime Families and within this wandering family-based coalition, they're raising some fantastic kids. [5]

The family makes a practice of welcoming all nature of diverse and interesting people to their fire. By doing so, John believes that they're building a childhood for their kids that places them "in firsthand contact with the issues our country is grappling with today." He's just one of the parents we've met who are making an inspiring choice to be active participants in the most essential and beautiful relationship of their lives. These kids will be the society builders of tomorrow. I'm convinced that it'll be a more inclusive world because their parents choose to provide them with the experience of sharing the fire of community through travel.

Commonalities in Choice and Necessity

While there is sometimes a correlation between socioeconomic status and RVing, I'm most interested in the commonalities between those who call an RV home by choice and those who live in one out of necessity. A sense of belonging is a universal longing. I believe anyone who's living in an RV by necessity has the same longing for connection and inclusion as everyone else. It would be easy to empathize with the person traveling with very modest resources and dismiss the needs of the person who rides in style. We may have different budgets, but no matter our means, we need that connection to others. Lacking it, we all suffer from a deep lonesome longing.

Are the characteristics that historically defined geographical *root communities* the same or similar for the mobile community? I believe that they are. The strong sense of connection starts with people learning one another's personal history. You will notice that if you stay a few days in a new park, you will meet your neighbors who are often eager to share the backstory of their journey. There is a mutual protectiveness that's quick to develop with campers. You will find campers looking out for one another, helping each other by assisting with set- up, watching pets and generally being a good neighbor in a small space.

We had to ask a man in an adjacent campsite to move his car so that we could pull out. He was the very spirit of generosity when he summoned it up by saying, "Anything you need. That's what we're all here for. To help each other." When you're living in such close proximity to each other, being kind is a matter of practical necessity as well as good-heartedness. If you're wise, you'll come to count on the exchange of knowledge and information from big-hearted RVers who always are willing to stop and help out a fellow roadie in distress. The Beatles were right. "I get by with a little help from my friends."

The size and value of an RV does not correlate to how communal or isolated the owner might be. For instance, a retired couple with the half-million-dollar coach may be quite a bit lonelier than the twenty-somethings in the retrofitted Volkswagen bus. The amenities included in some of the new models may enhance entertainment but increase isolation. While folks are watching dish TV in the Lazy-Boy recliners inside the comfort of their air-conditioned unit, they're not out and about meeting people. Our society places a high value on privacy and self-sufficiency. We value a private home, our own mode of transportation and the means to take care of ourselves without dependency. The high-end motor coaches certainly provide all of that. The challenge is to balance our desire for independence with our need for community. I have talked with folks who are traveling the country in the coach of their dreams and yet they feel alienated and lonely.

Meanwhile, the young folks in the van are dining at a picnic table or walking about by necessity. They're walking to the restroom for a shower, cooking over the fire, hiking with the dog and generally in closer proximity to other people. They have an increased likelihood of meaningful chance encounters because they're outside their unit more and naturally interacting with people. I see no distinction between the needs of the financially fortunate who full-time by choice and the needs of those who have taken up the lifestyle out of necessity. We all long to belong.

Maybe your own situation is pointing you to a life on the road more out of necessity than choice. Either way, you must still pass through the same process of transition and letting go. You still need to find community in wandering because the longing for interaction with others is a common factor for all of us. Everyone needs that very same thing: some degree of social interaction and the safety-net of connections. We need each other on the road, whether we're there by choice or necessity.

In our travels, Arnie and I have met many fascinating folks with inspiring stories of both choice and necessity. Each campground that we visit is a temporary home to an enclave of people with rich life experiences and tales to trade. I'm deeply grateful to all the people of goodwill who we've encountered along the way for their willingness to freely share their knowledge and experience with us. Our wandering community has given us new friends from all over the country. We're so grateful that our journeys have intersected and knowing them continues to enrich us in so many meaningful ways.

[1] https://www.investopedia.com/articles/economics/09/subprime-market-2008.asp

[2] https;//www.jessicabruder.com/nomadland-ii

[3] https://ditchingsuburbia.com/blog/rv-families-homeless

[4] https://www.coalitionforthehomeless.org/what-can-i-do-today-to-help-a-homeless-child/

[5] https://www.fulltimefamilies.com/

Chapter Nine
Creating and Sustaining Community

*"I think tolerance and acceptance, and love is
something that feeds every community."*
- Lady Gaga

The wandering community is fluid, a constant flow of new
names and faces. You meet interesting people and then you both
move on to continue your own itineraries. But you will inevitably
encounter some folks with whom you want to keep in touch
because you clicked on some level. You will know these folks
when you meet them. Maybe you respond to the world alike,
laugh at the same things, or enjoy an endless chat about the same
topic. Perhaps you see the logic in the same argument or perspective. Whatever it is that made you click in the first place, it is easy
to interact and communicate with them, making a sustained
friendship more likely.

Creating and maintaining connections as you wander is vital to
your very health and well-being. Studies have shown that a lack
of social relationships puts people at more significant health
risks than obesity, smoking, or high blood pressure. Not only
our happiness, but our health depends on making and keeping
relationships with others. There is a compelling body of research that shows a clear link between loneliness and increased
rates of mortality.

Dr. Emma Seppala of the Center for Compassion and Altruism
Research and Education of Stanford Medicine [1] says, "People
who feel more connected to others have lower levels of anxiety
and depression. Moreover, studies show they also have higher
self-esteem, greater empathy for others, are more trusting and

cooperative and as a consequence, others are more open to trusting and cooperating with them. In other words, social connectedness generates a positive feedback loop of social, emotional and physical well-being."

It was all over the news in 2018 when Theresa May, the Prime Minister of the United Kingdom, appointed a ministerial position on loneliness tasked with building community. Tracey Crouch holds the position of Loneliness Minister and her office helps to combat the country's chronic loneliness problem. In our own country, loneliness has been labeled with epidemic status, making it eligible for public health intervention. As yet, there have been no major government initiatives to combat this issue.

I believe that we can each be a force in shaping our health through community connections. When we transition to mobile living and leave behind our familiar relationships, it is even more vital that we create new ones. The social support that we give and receive is the best medicine to improve our health. Without a circle of friends and support around us, we are at risk of isolation, marginalization and loneliness.

Keeping Community

But we cannot sit back and wait for community to happen. Creating and preserving valued interpersonal connections is an active process and thus I think of it as keeping community. It isn't passive. It's a verb; to *keep community*. And the heart of keeping community is preservation. We preserve what is precious to us; we protect what we create. In traditional social groups, we attend to our close family and friendships by visiting in person, chatting on the phone and connecting on social media. We send birthday cards and take note of life's benchmarks such as graduations, weddings and new babies. We express our empathy when our friends experience illness, divorce, or loss in their lives. You have tended to your root community with care and concern. Like all relationships, wandering fellowship needs the same care and concern to keep it vital and healthy.

We have acquired some quick techniques for preserving initial contacts and helping them grow to be a part of our network of valued RVing relationships.

- You can exchange email addresses and send Facebook invites to folks you meet along the way when you feel a connection.

- Write down recipes and exchange them with other campers. Recipes are magic spells cast by kitchen witches. You can bring them home and craft them into a forever memory of someone you have met along your journey. When you make someone's recipe, text them and tell them that you are thinking of them and enjoying their Chicken Enchiladas for dinner (Carol) or their rhubarb jam (Carlie).

- Taking a quick photo and creating a contact in your smartphone is an excellent reminder of who you met and where you met them.

- We carry fun business cards with our names and contact information on them to hand out when we click with folks. On the back, we have a picture of our pets, making it easy for others to remember us as the people with the parrot.

Over a long holiday weekend, I met and interviewed a fascinating young lady who was camping next to us with her family. At the time that we met, Lana was a Divinity student at Vanderbilt University. She has a passion for farm to table gardening and eating, ethical sustainability and inclusion, particularly for people with developmental disabilities. She and her fiancé are room-mates with a young man with Downs Syndrome. Their loving friendship and natural support allow other students to include him in campus life in a variety of meaningful ways. The writings of Jean Vanier and the L'Arche Communities, [2] outline a concept where people with developmental disabilities live in friendship and fellowship with other students and this concept has inspired her. Lana is the kind of young person who gives me hope for the world. She is outward-looking and eager to tackle some of the pressing social problems facing us today. Meeting this amazing young woman gave me further insight into what constitutes an authentic community. Her enthusiasm and her good work prompted me to seek direction for this book on the topic of Intentional Community [3] and for that expanded perspective, I am appreciative.

When we cut our traditional ties and adopt an RV lifestyle, we create a state of marginalization. That may be a very new feeling for us and one we will need to work through intentionally. Everyone who travels is safer, healthier and happier when they actively connect to others. We know instinctively that a safety net is a good idea. Campers are very good at this. We have never struggled with hitching up or loading something heavy without the offer of assistance. If you look like you might be having a problem in a campground, it is almost inevitable that someone will approach with an offer to lend a hand. Helping others is an unspoken ethic among campers and it is often the starting point of conversation, which leads to a relationship. Relationship leads to community. If someone offers to assist you, by all means, accept. If someone needs assistance, by all means, offer it. Be intentional in this wandering world of ours.

There was one time when Arnie and I could have used a little assistance from fellow campers, but unfortunately at that time, no one happened to be around. It has made us more mindful of going camping in isolated areas where there is no support system at all. Why? Because stuff just seems to happen to us and when it does, a helping hand from other campers is most welcome.

We were heading out to go to one of our very favorite spots in Florida to spend a few days unwinding. Kissimmee Prairie Preserve is a remote state park that offers quiet solitude. It is a perfect place for reflection and relaxing. We have returned frequently and established connections with the hosts and campers who also love this special place. Some of my most insightful interviews for this book came from fellow campers at Kissimmee Prairie Preserve.

Sometimes the spirit of a place is so strong that you may sense an inner connection. Particular places exude a presence that we can hardly find words to describe. It's so much fun to explore new places, but it's also fun to return to our favorites. We all find our pearl in the oyster; that extraordinary place that speaks to us personally and becomes "our place." For us, that place is Kissimmee Prairie Preserve. It has an immense whispering that blows across the prairie and draws us back year after year. Here we have met many people to add to our circle of friends. From this special place, we have practiced actively keeping community, staying in touch with many folks we met there over the years. The voices of places that speak to you now will become sweet and enduring memories that you will cherish someday.

Locked and Loaded

Arnie and I value the company of others when we are camping. We enjoy sharing a campfire with new friends and old, swapping travel tales. So, it is puzzling how the two of us managed to get ourselves into such a stressful camping situation on one memorable visit to Kissimmee Prairie Preserve. We were still working at the time, not yet retired and very much looking forward to a lovely long weekend away from the phone calls and emails.

Consider this a cautionary tale about the value of camping in the company of others. It is also pretty darn funny…now. The mess we got ourselves into that night had a lot to do with the fact that it was very early in the camping season. Our choice to camp where we were the only people at this very remote location was another factor. It also may have had something to do with the beer.

Like many beer-related situations that folks get themselves into, this one is funny now. Not so funny then. We traveled down to the Fort Drum, Florida area, entered the preserve and set up our little unit Dinky Doo for the night in a lovely site across from the bathhouse. The weekend was meant to be a brief respite with no cell service or Wi-Fi. None of my crazed condo customers could get a hold of me for a whole long weekend. We settled into the camp chairs to unwind. It was off-season and hot, so a beer sounded ever so refreshing after setting up camp in the oppressive humidity. Except for the hoot owl in the tree over-head, it was just the two of us and we were looking forward to some togetherness.

Now, Arnie will have an occasional beer, but I hardly ever make this my beverage of choice. However, as I mentioned, it was Florida HOT. As dusk began to descend, I popped open a cold one for each of us. The first one went down well, so I hopped up, went inside and got us both another one. And then another. By now, the world is an exceedingly beautiful place, we are in love, there is no phone and no other campers. We can sleep late tomorrow morning, but for right now, the stars are out in a magnificent dark sky and life is good.

We finally got sleepy and I stood up to let the dogs out of the trailer one last time before we called it a night. It was time to retire to the comfort of our snug bed. Clamoring up out of the camp chair, I zigzagged towards the door, grabbed the handle and pulled. Oops, I must be doing something wrong. I tried again, summoning some focus through the beer haze.

"Release the handle and pull you drunken idiot," I counseled myself. "Take a deep breath and just pull." I drew breath, focused, snagged the door handle and pulled. It was locked.

"Arnie, the trailer's locked." I reported with only a slight hint of rising panic.

Arnie swatted a gnat and stirred in his chair. "How did you do that?" My husband has a gift for saying just the wrong thing at the right time.

"How did I do that?" I queried testily.

Arnie is not one to avoid the truth. "Well, you're the one who's been fetching the beer all night."

Noting my look, he quickly changed tactics and moved away from facts to something more productive. He moved directly to problem-solving.

"Just get the spare key out of the truck."

Having the solution in hand, instant relief flooded over me now as I zigzagged to the truck, reached for the door handle and pulled. I nearly fell over backward. It was locked too.

"Arnie, the truck's locked too."

Now back to facts. The RV is locked. The truck is locked. The cell phone, which has no reception anyway, is locked inside with the truck keys. We are alone because there are no other people foolish enough to camp off-season in this remote location. The rangers' office won't open until nine o'clock tomorrow morning. The two dogs are inside doing the Potty Dance. The mosquitoes are coming out in swarms and we taste good. I now took a crack at the facts myself.

"We're so screwed."

We desperately circled the Dinky Doo to identify our options. We hated to cut through the canvas on the ends and we had no sharp object anyway. We could gnaw our way through it, but dentistry is so expensive. Our dogs are not tall enough to flip the latch like Lassie, so they are no help. Not one window was cracked open. What are we going to do?

Arnie is not the cussing type, but this one called for some expression of frustration, so he kept channeling his dad's favorite cuss. Dad Jaquith kept this one just for exceptionally dire situations and never abused it for minor dilemmas.

"Son of a whore. Son of a whore. Son of a whore!"

Evidently, it was more effective if repeated three times in a row with a slight pause between the phrases. Part of the protocol is also to raise the volume from the first stanza to the third. I am sure there was alchemy involved and I now consider this epitaph to be an incantation of sorts. My wizard husband uttered the magic words three times over and voila, he had a bright idea.

"Check the cargo bay. Maybe it's unlocked."

I hustled over, grasped the handle and lifted it. The owl hooted encouragement overhead.

"Son of a whore, it's open."

The family magic had worked and we now had hope. Quite sobered up from the adrenaline of it all, we dragged everything out of the cargo hold and pounded out the supports holding up the inside bench seat with a hammer. Surveying the less than cavernous opening, I decided that it would be best for me to try to wiggle in first. Surely I would fit better. Wrong. My hips would not go past the first 2 x 4. After he extricated me, Arnie took over and once again muttered the magic words as he dove headfirst into the narrow space.

I watched him twist and squirm until he miraculously disappeared into the void. Somehow, he managed to squeeze himself up and inside, all the while being greeted and licked in the face by two thrilled little pups. To this day, we do not understand how he did it, but we do not question the power of the family magic. Seeing that door swing open was such sweet relief. But the sweetest relief is the knowledge that magic does exist and all you need to do to access the spell is to channel your dad.

This episode reminds us that as much as we admire the boondockers of the world, being part of a camping collective offers both security and safety. Call us chicken, but we have not been big enthusiasts of solo camping since. Now we pretty much stick to choosing locations where we can keep community with other travelers who could serve as a backup if needed. When we find ourselves confronted with adversity and hardships it can momentarily shake our will to continue. But sitting around a campfire with fellow wanderers helps us to refocus on our ability to adapt and find meaning in the kinship of the mobile community.

Safety in Numbers

There are well-established organizations that specialize in helping RVers to keep community. I would encourage anyone who is considering going full-time to research and join one of the travel clubs. These organizations provide support and services for the basic needs such as; roadside assistance insurance, mail-forwarding, campground discounts and reviews. Escapees [4] is an excellent resource. We particularly enjoy this membership for its special interest groups that make it easy to stay in touch with like-minded folks. Their BOF groups (for "birds of a feather") span a wide variety of interests within the mobile community.

An online search will quickly reveal that there are numerous options when it comes to travel clubs. Research the benefits that each one offers and compare them carefully to make sure that you choose the one that most closely meets your needs. There are many possible benefits and their prices vary widely. There is no point in paying for more than you need, but be sure to join the club that fits your unique needs. Be sure to check reviews also. There are also terrific forums online where you can learn from other seasoned travelers. YouTube [5] is an invaluable resource for specific information on nearly any travel topic. Some of the presenters support their travel habits with their well put together broadcasts and we enjoy following a number of them.

Staying Open

So how do you make those initial connections without feeling awkward or creepy about approaching new people? Especially if you are traveling solo or if you are an introvert, it may even be anxiety-producing. First, keep an open mind. You are going to meet different people from all over the world that you might never have a chance to talk with back in your root community. Differences such as age become irrelevant and people will surprise you over and over with their willingness to meet you halfway in a conversation.

If you can provide context for a conversation, it will happen naturally. Remember what I said about interviews often starting with where folks came from geographically? Put a sign out in front of your campsite with your name and your root community. You see these signs in every campground. These signs are one of the first things that go up when folks arrive and start to set up. Your sign will act as an ice breaker and start conversations with no effort at all on your part. Our sign says, Arnie and Barb Jaquith, Conyers, Georgia. It allows anyone who walks past our site to know our name and our home territory. Often people will stop by and ask questions about where we live or share that they too have been to the greater Atlanta area. The sign also has pictures of our animals and a catchphrase: Respect All Creatures. Folks who are out walking their dogs might be inclined to pause for a doggy meet and greet when they see we are animal lovers too.

Before we even speak a word, we have given anyone who would like to approach us some opening information about us. Fellow campers know we are traveling with a parrot and they can hear Cracker whistling. They know the breeds of dogs we own and they have a hint of our world view from our catchphrase. We have provided a lot of clues to who we are. Because we provided a context, people feel more relaxed and confident in approaching us and chatting for a bit.

Building Community Through Music

Music is a universal language that you can employ to find connections while you are traveling. One of our favorite places to visit is the Crooked Road music trail in Virginia. We have returned here many times to drink in the raw and keening power of the mountain music that we love so much. It is music that you learn to wear in layers as you return to it time and again to experience it. Some of our favorites are the oldest songs, known as "crooked tunes" due to their irregular measures. These songs gave the music trail its name and they speak to our hearts. Along the Crooked Road, we have made connections that developed into friendships and we love staying in touch with others who are interested in our country's musical heritage. There is no better way to make memories and build community than to seek out some live music and go listen in the warm company of friends.

In addition to the music, we love listening to the stories that the performers often tell between songs. The stories also bring people into community and tell us much about Appalachian traditions, folklore and people.

One night, a group of us camping friends attended a small concert with two wonderful older gentlemen well known on the mountain music and bluegrass scene. Bobbie Patterson has been playing with his musical partner Willard Gayheart for 39 years. The duo is known as The Fiddle and the Plow and when listening to their stories, it was sometimes hard to tell where the line between truth left off and storytelling began.

Bobbie gave our group of friends a good laugh that night with a story about a time when an old friend from Galax had to enter a nursing home. Bobbie knew his old buddy had always enjoyed his music over all the many years they had known one another, so he took his guitar over to the home to play some of the old songs for his friend. After Bobbie played and sang for about an hour, he packed up and got ready to depart. He wished his friend well and said, "I hope you get better."

His friend grinned. "I hope you do too."

Gaylord told a story about a visitor to the area who stopped off at one of the roadside mountain springs to get a cold drink of water. As he approached the spring, he noticed a slightly rumpled old local woman with tobacco stains running down both sides of her smile. She offered him her gourd to dip himself a drink. His mind raced as he pondered how to solve this awkward situation. How could he be gracious and not hurt Granny's feelings? He examined the gourd and noticed that the long thin handle was hollow. The visitor gratefully took the gourd from Granny, turned it upside down, wrapped his lips around the long handle and drank deeply. He handed the gourd back. "Thank you kindly, Ma'am."

Granny grinned a knowing grin. "You're welcome. Isn't it funny that you drink from that gourd just like me?"

Another excellent way to meet new people on the road is to volunteer. There are countless ways to get involved as a volunteer wherever you travel. The state and federal parks welcome volunteers and value the work that they do to maintain the natural resources. The Army Corps of Engineers maintains recreational areas that serve the public and they also welcome volunteers and can offer an enjoyable experience as well as providing hook-ups and amenities while you serve. Habitat for Humanity is a worthwhile endeavor and a variety of animal rescue groups need hands-on assistance too. Whatever your passion, you can find it on the internet and lend a hand. Do your research well, join one of the Facebook pages that provide reviews so that you know what you are getting into and benefit from the prior experience of other volunteers.

By far, the most important tip for beginning to establish your wandering network is to stop worrying. Most people who travel are open-minded to meeting new people. You do not need to be a witty conversationalist or an extrovert, just be who you are. Most people are going to be happy to meet and talk to you. After all, you must be pretty darn cool to have decided to wander full time.

So I encourage you to put in the time and effort to keep community as you wander. String all of these people and places together as you would thread colored beads on a necklace. You will wear this for the rest of your life. It will bring you great joy and sincere pleasure to conjure back your travels and the network you built along the way. Take lots of pictures of people and places. Take a sketchbook to the mountains and a journal to the beach; be a poet to your own experience. Gather small treasures like feathers and stones and save them in a box; they may be a summoning spell for you later. Memories and reminders of your journeys may be a tonic to your soul when life asks you to seek another path. Images are potent and can re-enchant our lives.

Sometime in the future, the memories that you created might be your renaissance. They may help you rediscover a time when you made a life-changing decision to live a season of life wandering in mobile community.

[1] http://ccare.stanford.edu/uncategorized/connectedness-health-the-science-of-social-connection-infographic/

[2] https://www.larcheusa.org/who-we-are/

[3] https://www.ic.org/

[4] https://www.escapees.com/

[5] https://www.youtube.com/

Chapter Ten
Chance Encounters

"Call it coincidence, destiny, fate, kismet- in one moment, lives can collide and change forever. Yet chance encounters aren't necessarily accidental; in fact, you can make your own luck by opening yourself to the world."
- Benn Sherwood.

There is a school of thought that every person on our planet is connected with someone else through just six other people. Six degrees of separation is the theory that all of us are only six or fewer social connections away from one another. It was originally a theory of Frigyes Karinthy in 1929 and later popularized in a 1990 play written by John Guare. [1] In everyday terms, six degrees of separation explains our small shrinking world. From our own experience, it seems plausible, as we are always meeting folks who share some familiar people and places with us. If you sit by the fire long enough and talk with people, you will eventually discover someone you both know in common. It truly is a small world and we have learned to be very deliberate in seeking out what we share in common with the people.

Soon after retiring from the corporate rat race, my husband Arnie and I hit the open road intending to seek interesting *chance encounters* along the way. We were on the lookout for contacts with people that we might never meet if we did not end up at the same place at the same time by chance. Chance encounters would become our tongue-in-cheek way of reminding ourselves that we are never really in control of what happens next in life. We knew that most of the people and places that we were going to meet and get to know would cross our path purely through serendipity. That meant we would be prudent to stay alert and recognize a great opportunity when it came along.

All of my interviews for this book started as a result of chance encounters when our journey intersected with fascinating fellow travelers. We kept our antenna up for great conversation and company and the information flowed from there. Some of those chance encounters were one-time connections and some of those folks have remained a valued part of our traveling tribe. And some prove out the concept of six degrees of separation. We experienced just that one night, in a campground along the Crooked Road [2] when Arnie noticed that the Road Trek van across from us had a New Hampshire plate on it.

He called over to the couple sitting at the picnic table. "What part of New Hampshire do you call home?"

"Campton, a little town in the White Mountains." My jaw dropped. I grew up in Campton. It was my root community from age nine to twenty-one when I left home to be married.

We walked over and introduced ourselves and then chatted for a bit. This delightful couple was on the way home to our original home state of New Hampshire. As we swapped stories, it turned out that Selma and Coke's son is married to the daughter of my childhood babysitter, Ginny. Ginny's younger sister, Rosie, was my best friend all through grade school, high school and college and on to this day. I could not wait to text Rosie and tell her who I was talking with at that very moment. Before they left early the next morning, we enjoyed some blueberry pancakes together and pledged to drop in on them at their son's Campton Coffee Shop this summer when we go to visit Rosie. This chance encounter was an extraordinary example of six degrees of separation.

I think of chance encounters as my job when I am traveling. It is my job to find a reason to meet and learn from new people, so I make it a point to talk with strangers. I deliberately challenge myself to dare to be in the world and learn through these chance encounters how deep my faith in people can go. I also realize that chance encounters can be related to places, not just people. There can be wonders galore waiting for you that are not marked on the map.

We think about our chance encounters as falling into two separate categories. There are those one-time meetings with folks who are interesting characters or someone we could learn something new from. These are the encounters that we enjoy in the moment and often remember fondly for the amusement or the wisdom that they offered when we met. And then there are the chance meetings with people and places that we will choose to preserve. These are the locations and folks who eventually become part of our wandering network, people that we can go to for friendship and advice, or places that we will return to time and again.

We value and appreciate both the one-time encounters as well as those that go on to be sustained friendships. We do love to keep an eye out for characters, though. It keeps the wandering life interesting. The trick is to keep in mind that you are not in any terrible hurry. The origin of most chance conversations is curiosity and fascination with something or someone. Folks are sometimes hesitant to engage in conversation with a stranger, so we have to take time, be patient and let it emerge. This is how and where belonging starts, one chat, one encounter at a time.

A Swampy Encounter

One unforgettable character that we met on a trip to the Big Cypress Swamp was Kelly. In this case, we met a memorable character and discovered an equally remarkable place.

Kelly was the night security guy at a fishing destination called Trail Lakes Campground embedded deep in the Ochopee swamp. It was also the setting of a roadside America attraction that just seemed too curious to miss. I had the bright idea that it would be a hoot to visit the Skunk Ape Research Headquarters [3] on our way to a birding festival in the Florida Keys. I have a penchant for roadside America, so how could we not stop by to try to catch a glimpse of the Skunk Ape, the Big Cypress Swamps' equivalent of Bigfoot?

Against Arnie's better judgment, we took a twenty-mile detour to this esteemed establishment. We both harbor a hearty sense of adventure, but this place exceeded even our wildest expectations. It is not for the faint-of-heart. Upon checking in, the pre-teen in charge of the office told us to go through the gate and stop at the first campsite on the left, honk the horn and the security guard would direct us to our campsite. We did as instructed and pulled up in front of the tiniest and oldest Airstream trailer I have ever seen. We honked and waited. Time passed and we sounded the horn again. After a long couple of minutes, the door flew open and a rather rotund bleary-eyed fellow lurched from the ancient sardine tin to greet us. He was wearing a big grin and a ratty pair of boxers. It is pretty hot here, but the beer in his fist probably helped to alleviate any discomfort.

Kelly slurred us a warm welcome as he climbed aboard a 40-year-old ATV. "Hi folks, I'm Kelly, your security guard."

He cranked it up, waited for it to backfire a couple of times and then drove off, waving for us to follow the cloud of whatever noxious concoction that thing runs on. With warm swamp hospitality, Kelly pointed us to the two muddy ruts that marked our campsite. "If you folks need anything in the night, just yell loud or shoot off a couple of rounds." With that comfort and reassurance, he left and we set up camp.

The campground was a shantytown fish camp, but its' setting in the glades made it a treasure. Our campsite was about thirty feet from the edge of the actual swamp itself and had a wild beauty. It is a place for ambling, albeit carefully. Here in the swamp, it is prudent to tread judiciously and watch where you are walking. If you go quietly and be still, you will find a vibrant ecosystem full of the most diverse bird and animal species to be found anywhere. Arnie and I have a fascination with reptiles, but to see them in their habitat you have to move unobtrusively. At dusk, the gators gazed at us out of the sawgrass and grumped at our doorstep.

Big Cypress is the perfect place to do walking meditation, absorbing the tranquility and serenity of the area. We were glad for our policy of staying put for a minimum of three or four days to feel the consciousness of each location. While we did not catch a sighting of the Skunk Ape, we saw an abundance of other creatures that are found only in the everglades. Edward O Wilson, the famed Harvard entomologist, wrote: "Humanity is exalted not because we're so far above other living creatures, but because knowing them well elevates the very concept of life."

A Recipe for Connection

Some of our chance encounters have developed into cherished friendships. We have connected with some dear people that we keep in touch with and visit along the way. They are camping acquaintances who have become beloved and cherished friends. Michael and I met over thirty years ago camping across from one another for a whole summer in Ogunquit, Maine, where our summer sites faced one another. We bonded instantly and nearly thirty years later, he is still one of my closest friends. We have supported one another through thick and thin and no distance has every interrupted our friendship. When we get together, we reminisce about days past and it often has to do with some hilarious situation we shared camping.

Michael and I spent many weekends experimenting with new recipes and enjoying meals with friends. The fact that we were cooking in travel trailer kitchens didn't dampen our enthusiasm in the least. We had great fun making good food with good friends. Our circle of friends grew over seven summers spent in this special place where we enjoyed pot lucks, campfire dinners, fish fries and birthday cakes. Food and friends came together to create lasting relationships that I treasure to this day.

Michael is my foodie friend. You know the kind. He has impeccable taste, champagne taste on a beer budget. He can pull off a gourmet meal in a small RV kitchen and make it look easy. He's the Julia Child of RVing. Ogunquit means "beautiful place by the sea," and many great fish markets populate the town featuring an abundance of fresh Atlantic seafood. Seafood figured heavily in our weekend menus when we got together to cook.

One memorable weekend, Michael decided to whip up a special meal for a nice fellow he had met recently. Meaning to impress, Michael bought all of the ingredients for an exquisite traditional Maine meal. I inquired what was to be on the menu for his date. "It's the first date. Of course, it has to be lobster."

I was sitting on my deck quietly reading a book when I heard Michael call over to me from his adjacent site. "Barbara, I've got a question. Can you flambé lobster in a non-stick pan?"

I pondered the question for a moment. Frankly, at the time, I was not under the impression that my dear friend could afford to flambé anything in any pan, but I guess that wasn't the point. Putting aside all of the sarcastic quips that were running through my head, I responded authoritatively, "Sure, I don't know why not."

"Okay, thanks." Michael disappeared into the RV again. I could hear pots and pans clanging; he was clearly on a mission to create a memorable meal. The object of his attention arrived shortly, waved to me and also disappeared inside. I sat on my deck, envisioning the lovingly prepared delicacy that they would soon enjoy over a bottle of fine wine. Everything was in place for a successful first date on a lovely summer evening.

Suddenly, the door to Chef' Michael's flew open, banging flat against the siding of the RV with a metallic crash that drew the attention of everyone around- including those resting quietly in the cemetery next door. I looked up just in time to see Michael fly through the air in a pose from Swan Lake with that non-stick pan extended far in front of him. A firestorm rose from the pan skyward, kissing the canvas of the awning. Michael's feet never touched the steps; he just levitated through the air and landed at a dead run over to the fire pit. I watched in both wonder and horror as he threw about a hundred dollars' worth of flaming crustacean into the dirt.

Apparently, when Michael reached the step where alcohol meets a sizzling pan, a giant wall of flame rose up like a David Copperfield magic trick. I think the trick is called Tornado of Fire and people pay big money for tickets to see this spectacle in Vegas. Michael did it for free that day. French waiters can pull off this culinary trick to impress diners at fancy French restaurants, but it was never meant to be executed in the confines of a trailer kitchen. At the moment, when he added the vodka to the pan and lit the match, the alcohol had ignited in a flare that instantly reached Biblical proportions, ending all hope of a tasty meal. Memorable, yes. Tasty, not so much.

The good news is that the trailer did not burn down in an inferno of gourmet spices and expensive lobster. The bad news is that Michael's camping friends have never let him forget this story. It is stories and memories like this that keep community. In their retelling, stories rekindle friendships and restoke shared memories of good – and sometimes exciting- times with dear friends.

Every new person that we meet along the journey is a potential new member of our mobile community and meeting new people lets us practice the spiritual principles that help guide us. Respect is a central principle that we try to practice when we are wandering. In our travels, we try to approach each chance encounter as an opportunity to meet another person we can learn from if we are respectful of their right to hold an opposing point of view or lifestyle from our own. When we come to a new campground, we hang out our sign that says, "Respect for All Creatures." as an open invitation to converse with us respectfully.

Chance encounters place us in close proximity to other people and their "home" property. When you are camping, you become temporary neighbors with people from all walks of life and many different places. Inevitably, you will encounter folks who follow a different path and who may hold a very different worldview from your own. Sometimes when we first meet people, we may form an impression of them which may be wrong or incomplete, but we do our best to keep talking until we find common ground. We try to be open enough to get to know them better, to let them reveal other sides of their character and to become aware of their better qualities. Once we find our common ground, we honor those qualities. The Buddha said that the ability to feel respect is a great blessing. We have been mightily blessed so far in our travels by being respectful.

A Two-Wheeled Encounter

Our meeting with Nigel was an especially exciting chance encounter for Arnie. Nigel is a long-distance adventure bicyclist with a fascinating story. Arnie was a long-distance bicyclist himself for many years, so I turned the interview over to him as they had so much in common. Nigel is from Preston, England, about 40 miles out of Manchester. He had recently flown into Dulles to begin the Transamerica [4] and was planning on biking about 50 miles per day over 86 days. We met him at Natural Chimneys campground, a stop-off to shelter over on a chilly rainy night. Nigel was carrying a copy of Walt Whitman's Leaves of Grass [5] with him. We asked what his favorite quote was and he replied, "Afoot and lighthearted I take to the open road. Healthy, free, the world before me." Arnie enjoyed hearing about his travels on a bike through England, Spain and Norway before he tackled the States. We had to respect his stamina and his enthusiasm for seeing the world in this most intimate way. We felt sorry that the weather was being very inhospitable to him in his little pop-up tent, so Arnie later went over with a bowl of hot vegetable soup, an egg salad sandwich and rhubarb crisp. We hope that the hot meal reinforced his statement that, "Americans are the friendliness and most welcoming people in the world."

An Incredible Hulk Encounter

It takes all kinds and we sure do enjoy most of our chance encounters as we wander. Always and forever, I keep foremost in my mind Plato's advice that we should "Be kind, for everyone you meet is fighting a harder battle." But, once in a while, we end up camped next door to someone we might not enjoy so much. On one such weekend, we found ourselves accidental neighbors with Biker Man and Hulk.

Hulk is an English bulldog puppy who has his owner completely wrapped up. Hulk's person is a stereotypical biker who travels about in a Class A rig with his motorcycle in tow. Oddly enough, Leather-clad Biker Man talks baby talk to Hulk- constantly. This former tough guy keeps up a running commentary on Hulk's wants and needs. He serves as the translator interpreting for others who do not speak bulldog. Biker Man is that campsite neighbor that you do not want to be beside. He continually visits with his dog and talks of nothing else. No one can divert him from the topic of Hulk, the wonder bulldog.

We first met Biker Man when he exited his toy hauler trailer and headed in our direction with Hulk snorting and leading the way. "I know, Hulk, you want to visit the neighbors." That was our cue and, after a few days, we learned to head inside or look busy. If we were lucky, the conversation would be comparatively quick because Hulk had his business to do. We knew when this was the case because Hulks' translator would announce it. "I know, Hulk, you have to take a dump. Do you need to take a dump? Come on, Hulk, do you need to go?" As if we needed to be involved in the process, Biker Man would announce, "He likes to take his walk. Are you a good boy, Hulk? Come on, let's take a dump. Tell the neighbors to have a good day, Hulk and you'll visit later. He gets a treat after he takes a dump." As they departed for the dog walk area, Arnie shook his head and muttered. "Thanks for sharing,"

Our experience with Biker Man and Hulk aside, our chance encounters generally teach us to take the time to look for and find something unique to respect about all people and creatures. They make us feel at home wherever we are and form the basis of our wandering kinship group. As we travel and keep community, we are so grateful for all the people of goodwill who have entered our lives by way of chance.

Growing the Friendship Garden

Our wandering community has been sparked by chance encounters and then forged by shared campfires. Rob and Carol, Stan and Carlie were co-hosts with us during the summers at West

Hill Dam, a beautiful Massachusetts Army Corps of Engineers site. Rolling up our sleeves to be mutual stewards of a piece of land that we all cared about drew us close together in lasting friendships. Together we tended the pollinator gardens, maintained the trails and nurtured the seeds of curiosity about nature in young visitors. We planted flowers and gardens and shared the fruits of our summer labor with one another. Most of all, we planted kindness and connection.

We have also stayed connected with some of the student interns and the summer rangers who we first met at West Hill and it delights us to follow their interesting career paths and hear of their academic success. In particular, Sally and Rachel are brilliant young women who are contributing to the science and the ethics of preserving our environment. We are heartened by their commitment and activism to our world. We came together in friendship at shared potlucks and campfires organized by Ranger Viola, who we cherish for her many years of dedicated service as a ranger with the Army Corps of Engineers. She has shared her passion for the plant and animal world with thousands of Junior Rangers and taught water safety to school children in the neighboring towns. She is a rare gift in our lives. As a result of some chance encounters, we have been forged by the fire into friendship with some amazing people.

The connection that we made with Carol and Larry through our love of birds has blossomed into a bond that I could never have expected. Larry has so very kindly served as a cheerleader for this book and it would not have come into being without his valuable guidance and encouragement. Larry's assistance is a generosity and kindness I could never have expected, nor could I ever repay.

Michael, my foodie friend, has been seated at my virtual campfire for close to thirty years. Across the miles and the years, we have kept in touch with frequent phone calls that often start with his cheerful, "Hello, Dearie." Michael and I met at a seasonal campground in Maine, the same place I met Karen, who is the sister I never had. She and I have been best friends for close to thirty years also, loving one another through life's heartaches and triumphs. We have sat far into the middle of many nights, trying to reconcile our tragic losses and disappointments over a glass of wine. To think that merely sharing a fire could lead to friendships of this depth and duration is amazing.

And who could forget Traveling Pat? My sassy friend Pat embarked on a road trip at the age of eighty-six with her 87-year-old friend. They crossed the country in her car, tenting and couch surfing with friends scattered far and wide. Her indomitable spirit of adventure is inspirational. There are so many more folks met through chance encounters and I don't wish to leave anyone out. It is a joy and a privilege to share tender friendships around the fire with each of you.

Isn't it exciting to wonder who you will encounter and add to your own circle of friends as you travel about? There are people out there who need and want to make your acquaintance and having a chance encounter with them is your opportunity to make a difference in someone's life. As Fred Rogers said, "If you could only sense how important you are to the lives of those you meet; how important you can be to the people you may never even dream of. There is something of yourself that you leave at every meeting with another person.

[1] https://en.wikipedia.org/wiki/Six_degrees_of_separation

[2] https://www.smithsonianmag.com/travel/a-musical-tour-along-the-crooked-road-49549719/

[3] https://www.skunkape.info/

[4] https://www.goworldtravel.com/initiation-transamerica-bike-trail/

[5] https://poets.org/book/leaves-grass

Chapter Eleven
The Wanderlust

"Once a year, go someplace you've never been before."
- His Holiness the Dalai Lama

Arnie and I traveled half time for two years, easing into the lifestyle of full-timing. Each time we came off the road, we were glad to see our neighbors and friends and return to our land-based home. But it was never long before we were struck by the wanderlust calling us back to adventure and faraway places. We choose to respond to the call of the gypsy heart rather than resist and cultivate any immunity to it. It feels like it is in our very blood. I wondered if there is more to this strong urge to travel and how we have come to share it with so many people we meet in our travels. I wondered if there was a whole group of folks out there struck by the same restlessness as we have been and if so, why?

The wanderlust has always been with me. I have watched Ken Burns's series, *The National Parks: America's Best Idea* [1], at least three times all the way through. In each of the six episodes, filmed over six years, he takes us on an armchair tour of some of the most awe-inspiring locations from Alaska's arctic regions to Florida's everglades. Burns tours us through Acadia in Maine and Yosemite in California as he tells us the stories of the people who worked to saves these lands for our children and us. He reminds us of what makes America a great nation and inspires us to board the bus and get out there to see the land and meet the people in person. Watching any episode of this series ignites the wanderlust in me.

The writings of John Muir spark a similar fascination for me too. The Sierra Club maintains an online curated collection of his life's work entitled The John Muir Exhibit. [2] As you transition into full-time living on the road, you may find his writings inspirational and a good reminder of why you are re-engineering your lifestyle. Muir encourages you with his statement that "between every two pine trees there is a door leading to a new way of life."

An Unfulfilled Bold Journey

My first recollection of being struck by the wanderlust is when my dad and his best friend Larry built a rudimentary pop-up trailer from scratch. It was back around 1956 when I was six years old. Their homemade contraption was a chunky bulky contraption constructed out of plywood and perched on a steel bed. They painted it red with white letters on the side, announcing that it was the Bold Journey. They were going fishing in Canada and even then, as a six-year-old tomboy, I loved fishing. And I loved my dad. I handed him the hammer and picked up the nails off the ground. He patiently let me pound, paint and putter with him. I remember to this day the squeaking sound of the heavy hinged top when he hefted it aloft to reveal the finished product. Inside it was neatly packed with sleeping bags, a cook stove, fishing gear and firewood. It was my own Barbie's dream house and I was enchanted.

The anticipation was palpable and I could hardly wait to climb aboard and leave on our trip. But, Dad and Larry were very strategic in not telling me that this was a grown-up guys' only trip. My parents never announced that we were headed to get annual flu shots before we pulled into the doctors' yard either. It avoided the hysterics until the very last moment and did not drag out the suffering. I did not realize that I was not going until the day that Dad and Larry pulled out of the driveway, leaving me behind.

I vividly recall falling prostrate, sobbing on the pavement in our front yard as Bold Journey turned the corner of First Street and disappeared into the distance. That formative heartbreak would mean that I would grow up determined to never miss another Bold Journey again. Many years later, I spoke with both my dad and Larry about this transformational moment when the wanderlust awoke in my early childhood. Neither one remembered it. They were just two guys on a fishing trip who never looked in the rearview mirror. Now that is a philosophy I come by naturally.

The U.S. Femail Adventure

My own first Bold Journey would need to wait a few years. In my junior year of college, two girlfriends and I embarked on an adventure that was epic in our adolescent minds, even for the sixties. Today it seems rather tame, but back then, it was wild and adventurous to three fast friends who wanted to see some of the world.

Penny, Rosie and I pooled funds and purchased a retired mail delivery box van. My dad spent weekends and nights gutting and renovating the interior into a bunkhouse with storage. It was the reincarnation of his old Bold Journey and the sixties hippie equivalent of an RV. If he questioned the prudence of the three of us taking off for parts unknown in a mail truck, he never tainted our experience with parental angst or worry. We repainted the US Mail symbol on the rear of the van to read US FEMAIL and hit the open road. I remember departing with my grandmother, Mamie, wringing her hands in front of her house from the sure knowledge that this would be our eternal undoing.

It was a lifetime experience for three girls from a small town in New Hampshire who had never been much of anywhere. Despite the fear it struck in my grandmother's heart, off went the hippie chicks to see the country in a box truck with only AAA maps to guide us. Our karma must have been righteous because we met and stayed with some kind people who housed, fed and encouraged us in our quest. It was a first naive foray from home for us and the beginning of many between us. We traveled hither and yon. We celebrated Easter in a Philadelphia cathedral with Penny's minister friend. We welcomed the coming of spring in Shenandoah National Park with Gallo wine in a basket-wrapped bottle. And we hit the southernmost point of the United States when we visited Key West, where my vacationing parents treated us to a motel room for a night. In between, good people took us under their wings, shared their fire and showed us the land and their interpretation of what it was to be American in that distinctive decade.

The Plague of Curiosity

The wanderlust has never left me. I feel the call of new places like an ache in my soul and intense curiosity plagues me. I realize that there are plenty of people who never feel the urge to leave their homes, but I never understood why. They are content to stay where they came from and let the recliner transport them around the world via TV. In a fashion, I envy them their contentment in their space and their comfort with the familiar. At times I crave the predictable schedule, structure and rituals that work for them and wish I could relate.

Sometimes I think they may be the lucky ones because the wanderlust does not interrupt a comfortable life with its beckoning call. They cook fish on Friday and go to church on Sunday, Saturday night supper is beans and franks. Spring cleaning and putting the garden in after Memorial Day are all routines that keep the suitcase in the closet. I recognize the value of predictability and the comfort of knowing what comes next. *Home sweet home* works for most sane people.

Then there are the rest of us, the people whose contentment originates with change and not with the status quo. I keep the Travel Channel saved to favorites on the TV and always have a backpack fully loaded just in case a friend calls to go exploring on a hike. I have never succeeded in fully embracing the home-body lifestyle. Just as I start to settle in, I get bitten by the bug and off I go once again. I enjoy planning and packing for the next chapter, researching what waits around the next bend and who might be out there to meet. I unfailingly choose the car seat over the couch.

Why is it that some people need to move about instead of staying put? Is it wanderlust, a love of travel or regular old curiosity? For them, the thirst for exploring is unquenchable, no matter how many unique journeys they take. There is always something new to see, something different from the day to day norm and they need to reroot in the world of nature. These are the folks who enjoy day trips, but they also realize there is only so much to see in 24 hours. It is the trip to nowhere with the serendipitous find at the end that is fulfilling. It is the chance encounters that whisper to them, "Let's go down that back road there and see where it takes us."

A Species on the Move

Arnie and I have met so many people in our travels that are prone to wanderlust as we are and they share a similar story to our own. They are drawn to a life of wandering and are the happiest living the nomadic lifestyle. We wondered why. It turns out that scientists are asking this very same question.

"No other mammal moves around like we do," says Svante Paabo, a director of the Max Planck Institute for Evolutionary Anthropology in Leipzig, Germany, [3] where he uses genetics to study human origins. "We jump borders. We push into new territory even when we possess resources where we are. Other animals don't do this. Other humans either. Neanderthals were around hundreds of thousands of years, but they never spread around the world. In just 50,000 years, we covered everything. There's a kind of madness to it. Sailing out into the ocean, you have no idea what's on the other side. And now we go to Mars. We never stop. Why?"

What is behind this? It turns out that it may be the gift of ancestry that fuels the gypsy heart of folks like us. The foundation may originate in our genome. Scientists have identified a mutation that is a variant of a gene called DRD4 which regulates dopamine. Dopamine is a chemical brain messenger with a role in learning and reward. Researchers have tied this variant known as DRD4-DRD4-7R to curiosity and restlessness and roughly 20 percent of all humans are carriers.

Some studies tie DRD4-7R to human migration. Professor Chuansheng Chen of the University of California, Irvine, in 1999 found DRD4-7R more common in present-day migratory cultures than in settled ones. His work might support the idea that a nomadic lifestyle selects for the DRD4-7R variant. [4]

A separate study done by David Dobbs of National Geographic [5] supported these findings and provided a reason to draw the link to curiosity and restlessness, but specifically a passion for travel. According to Dobbs, the mutant form of the DRD4-DRD4-7R gene results in people who are "…more likely to take risks; explore new places, ideas, foods, relationships, drugs, or sexual opportunities." He went on to say that bearers of this gene, "…generally embrace movement, change and adventure."

Yale University's evolutionary and population geneticist Kenneth Kidd [6] is more cautious about this explanation. He was part of the team that discovered the DRD4-7R variant 20 years ago and is skeptical about overstating the link between DRD4-7R and exploratory traits. "You just can't reduce something as complex as human exploration to a single gene. Genetics doesn't work that way." He suggests that we might be better to consider how groups of genes might lay a foundation for wandering behavior. But he does not seem to entirely dismiss a genetic basis for the driving restlessness that some of us feel. He cautions a more likely scenario is that different groups of genes contribute to multiple traits. Some allow us to explore and others, possibly DRD4-7R drive us to do so. It seems it is not just the urge to travel and explore but also the ability. To travel takes not only the motivation to explore but also the motivation to create the means and the tools.

I believe that there is a nurture factor working alongside the nature factor in the psyche of some of us wanderers. I credit my grandfather Barta for bequeathing me the wanderlust. Barta read to me cover to cover from his collection of beautifully bound volumes of Aesop's fables. I can still feel the excitement of a young imagination transported to those other worlds. I have never lost the love of some of these children's literature greats and one of my all-time favorites is *The Wind in the Willows* by Kenneth Grahame.[7]

It is fascinating to listen to Grahame's character Toad describe his first "RV," and I can relate to his excitement. Those who have gone to an RV Expo or dealership looking for their first home on wheels will recognize themselves in Toad's enthusiastic description of his new purchase.

> *"There's real life for you, embodied in that little cart. The open road, the dusty highway, the heath, the common, the hedgerows, the rolling downs! Camps, villages, towns, cities! Here today, up and off to somewhere else tomorrow! Travel, change, interest, excitement! The whole world before you and a horizon that's always changing!*

And mind! This is the very finest cart of its sort that was ever built, without any exception. Come inside and look at the arrangements. Planned 'em all myself, I did."

Whatever side of the debate you come down on, we should thank all of the responsible folks lacking this gene for staying home and keeping the home fires burning. Meanwhile, we twenty-percenters jaunt out with reckless abandon, leaving them wringing their hands in the driveway like my poor grandmother.

Mamie's concern might not have been entirely ungrounded. Garret LoPorto is a counterculture activist, author and speaker.[8] He weighs in on the discussion with the opinion that carriers of this genetic variant might be "...incredibly resourceful, pioneering, creative and more predisposed for wanderlust. They also might be utterly out of control."

If gene theories offer some insight into the source of the passion that overtakes some of us when we pass an RV dealership, then maybe we should take just a moment to notice the dark side of any decision that is driven by passions and impulse. Gene theory offers a word of caution to those of us who are affected by wanderlust and who might be prone to making out of control decisions. I suffer from this myself and struggle with the temptation to skip all of the details and get on with the fun stuff. I'm impatient with the process and details and just want to get moving. But history tells me that tempering the restlessness with common sense and proper planning gives me a better long term result. If you are prone to the dark side too, I encourage you to answer the call of the wanderlust with discernment and to approach this life transition with appropriate planning and consideration.

A Cautionary Tale

With their kind permission, this is a great time to tell you about the experience of our dear friends Deb and Bert. Arnie and I are a few years ahead of them on the retirement timeline, but the four of us have spent endless hours talking and fantasizing about how much fun it would be to travel together after they retire in a few years. They are willing to share this cautionary tale as a lesson to all who answer the call of the wanderlust prematurely.

Roberta and Deb bought their first RV to spend weekends enjoying camping along Florida's beaches with friends. It seemed like a good idea to acquire their trailer before retirement and get some practice in. Besides, they were fevered with wanderlust and longing to get out there on some long weekends with friends.

They visited several dealerships and chose what they believed would be the perfect rig for them- a nifty twenty-five-foot towable trailer with a matching silver Toyota Tundra pick-up truck to complete the ensemble. The next few weekends were spent shopping and fully equipping the camper and truck. Soon it was time to take the new playhouse out for its maiden voyage. With all the rush of anticipation that accompanies a new adventure and a new toy, they loaded up their beautiful white fluffy Bichon Frise dogs Buddy and Cincy, a bottle of Jameson whiskey and other necessities and off they went to their reserved space at gorgeous Fort De Soto on Florida's west coast.

After a wonderfully relaxing weekend, they packed up and headed home. As we know, when you leave home on a weekend camping trip, all is rosy and you are in your happy place. The dogs are sparkling clean, the laundry smells like Febreeze and the food in the fridge is inviting. But when checkout time on Sunday rolls around, the dogs are full of sand, every stitch of clothing is smoky and the remnants of the food stink like aging leftovers. Also, the bottle of Jameson is empty and you forgot the Tylenol.

Bert and Deb departed camp and were driving home on busy Interstate 4, a bit tense from the Sunday afternoon traffic when the inevitable happened. About half an hour before they arrived at the storage facility to park, unhook and unload their trailer from its maiden voyage, the heavens opened up in a typical Florida afternoon torrential downpour. Now, after a nail-biting drive on the highway, they must back their unit into a space that was comparatively cavernous when they departed. But now, it is only half the original size thanks to the incompetent parking job on the part of the two big boats on either side of them. There is room, but barely.

Deb, who does the driving, must squeeze their trailer backward into a skinny reserved space in the pouring rain, without being able to hear Roberta's directions over the din of the rain, thunder and lightning. Visibility is limited to only what she can catch between the windshield wipers flying by on high. Did I mention that this is Deb's first crack at backing up? Not exactly a Zen moment to be sure.

They unhooked the sway bar through the wind and rain and did the bump and grind backward into the narrow space. They pushed through it and solved the problem. They are still not quite sure what that loud noise was or how that hole got punched into the bumper of the new truck and Deb's foot healed in a couple of weeks from dropping the hitch on it. But what is important is that they made it home, relationship relatively intact.

As funny as experiences like this may be, they do teach us valuable lessons. Deb and Roberta eventually decided that towing a trailer was not the best arrangement for them. They ultimately sold the truck and trailer and have decided to wait until they retire to commit to traveling when they will really have the time to relax and enjoy it. At that time, they plan to choose a smaller Class C Unit that will be easier and less stressful for them to drive and maneuver. The moral of the story is to choose both the right time and the right rig for your particular adventure.

Whose Dream Is It Anyway?

You will likely hear from friends and family that you have "caught the travel bug." It is just their way of framing something that they do not understand. You are not suffering from an infection or illness, nor are you a victim of an adverse condition. As you talk about your transition, you will encounter a few folks who perceive RVing as an alternative lifestyle that is inherently negative. They may be genuinely concerned for you and wonder why you would be so keen on jumping about with no stability. The thought of potentially having no secure income and pretty much no clue where you are going next is quite unsettling to them. Most will think that you will get it out of your blood after a while or grow out of it. But this is your dream, not theirs.

One helpful way to think about it is that you are a nomad among settlers. Listen to your calling and your need to explore even when those around you do not share that interest. You are not a fork dropped in the spoon drawer by mistake. If the time is right for you and you are ready, you are in good company and about to discover your own mobile community.

[1] http://www.pbs.org/nationalparks/

[2] https://vault.sierraclub.org/john_muir_exhibit/writings/

[3] https://www.eva.mpg.de/genetics/staff/paabo/cv.html

[4] https://www.newscientist.com/article/mg21028114-400-out-of-africa-migration-selected-   novelty-seeking-genes/

[5] https://www.nationalgeographic.com/magazine/2013/01/restless-genes/

[6] https://medicine.yale.edu/genetics/people/kenneth_kidd-2.profile

[7]https://lithub.com/the-wind-in-the-willows-isnt-really-a-childrens-book/

[8] https://www.huffpost.com/entry/surprising-way-your-neand_b_568455?guccounter=1

Chapter Twelve
One of Those Days

"When it's not always raining there'll be days like this. When there's no one complaining there'll be days like this. When everything falls into place like the flick of a switch. Well my mama told me there'll be days like this."
- Van Morrison

There is one reality of full-timing that is undeniable and that is the uncertainty associated with RVing. Anyone who travels in an RV will tell you that you will experience some degree of uncertainty each and every day. Can you get reservations? Can you fit into the site? What will the terrain be like and can your vehicle navigate it? What's that strange new clicking noise in the engine? When you are traveling and in new situations every day, nearly everything has some aspect of uncertainty about it and your problem-solving skills will need to be sharp. When you are faced with "one of those days", it is normal to feel a bit anxious and overwhelmed, but you are in good company. We all have those days.

My Arnie likes to putter around the RV, cleaning this, polishing that, repairing and maintaining the unit and the truck. Arnie is terrific at making things work better, smoother, more efficiently, so I try to accommodate his timing because I am aware that there is a real payoff. One day while I was preparing supper for the animal crew, he greased up the truck's hitch ball and the mount on Dinky Doo, lathering on the noxious black goo in thick globs. He did not mention to me that he had freshly greased the hitch, he just did it. The problem is that the hitch sticks right out of the back of the truck, where I needed to go for canned goods and supplies multiple times every day. In the short space of one hour, I managed to brush into the hitch, ruining two pairs of tan pants by smearing that grease all over both knees as I bumped against it trying to retrieve dog food. Two hours at the seediest Laundromat I have ever seen did not even come close to removing it. Worse than that, the neighbors in the next campsite stared at me aghast when I loudly exclaimed in frustration, "I hate your greasy balls."

Another one of those memorable days happened in Everglades National Park. One day, Arnie and I had just come out of the woods from a long hike and I spied a sign for a much-needed restroom. It was like an oasis in the desert and nature was calling. I needed a ladies' room and was willing to overlook the conditions. My theory on compost toilets is that all will be well if you don't look down. I employ denial to get through challenging situations such as this gigantic Petrie dish that was trying to pass for a ladies' room.

Hustling past the sign with the bullet hole in it, I carefully took the iPad I carry for identifying birds, plants and various crawly things and gently set it on the edge of the sink (the only relatively clean spot in the room) so that there could be no accidents. I could not help but notice that the walls were dripping with humidity and the floor was growing with greasy green swamp slime. I finished up, retrieved the iPad and gingerly walked towards the door with mincing steps across the slick wet floor. Then it happened. In a flash, my feet flew apart and forward, tossing me flat on my back in the muck, knocking the wind right out of my lungs. I slid across the floor, stopping like a hockey player when I collided with the wall. The tablet skimmed to the far side of the room like a flat stone over a pond leaving a track in the wet compost. The cell phone that I had in my back pocket popped out and took a trip of its own in the opposite direction. I laid there gasping for a moment, trying to determine what was bashed, broken or sprained. The yuck in my hair was not yet a consideration.

Gathering my wits about me, I determined that I was going to be sore but luckily intact and started to inch myself upright. But the old high school skiing injury to my knee screamed a caution. I knew I needed Arnie to come and haul me up. Boy, I just hated to yell for help, so I sat there for a bit, hoping to gather the strength to right the ship on my own. But this was the Big Cypress Swamp for Pete's sake. It was mucky and smelly and I was sitting in a room with a leaky compost toilet. I could not just continue to sit there and see what helpful reptile wandered in. I tentatively called for Arnie with no response. I pictured him off peacefully staring at birds in trees through binoculars while I lay mired in a blend of primeval toxins.

Finally, after an extended time, Arnie came looking for me, "Babe, are you in there?" he called politely around the ladies room corner. "Yes, I need help. I slipped and fell." He bounded in, surveyed the scene with me on the floor in a heap and our technology lodged in separate corners across the room. As I tearfully looked up for the heartfelt sympathy and concern I was expecting, he then did what any loving husband would do without even thinking about it. He exclaimed, "Oh my God! The iPad!"

I'll spare you the rest of the conversation or lack thereof. Suffice it to say that the iPad, the phone and I all survived. Somehow our relationship as well. This experience is one of those things that you laugh about later, not so much at the moment. We decided to put the incident to music and then sang it to the tune of She'll Be Coming Round the Mountain.

> *She'll be coming round the compost when she falls.*
> *She'll be sliding cross the floor when she falls.*
> *She'll be coming round the compost*
> *She'll be coming round the compost*
> *She'll be sliding round the compost when she falls.*

She'll be slipping in the yuck n' muck when she lands.
She'll be sliding across the yuck n' muck when she lands.
She'll be slipping and a sliding
She'll be slipping and a sliding
She'll be stirring up the compost when she lands.

Yee Ha!

Stress Busters

It's a given that there will be days that do not go as planned. We have found a few tried and true ways to prepare for and cope with those times. I hope some of these strategies might be helpful to you too.

- Keep to a sleep schedule. Try to keep a consistent bedtime and wake-up time with seven to eight hours of sleep every night. Honor a nightly routine such as listening to a meditation app on your smartphone or try a white noise machine.

- Establish a predictable schedule of eating, exercising, potty breaks and bedtime for the pets. The last call just before dark avoids late-night wildlife encounters in strange places (think skunks).

- Keep in touch with friends and family with a weekly skype call. Staying informed about what is actually happening at home keeps your imagination in check.

- Reach out to other experienced travelers to hear their stories about their experiences. Our fellow roadies are a rich source of common sense and problem-solving.

- Eat healthy and in moderation. Go home once a year to visit your primary for an annual check-up so that you keep on top of any medical issues.

- Arrange ahead to schedule your mail and medication deliveries or arrange for a nationwide pharmacy where you can refill anywhere (Wal-Mart, Costco, Sam's Club, etc.).

- Get a bit of exercise every day. Take a short walk after you are hooked up and ready to depart just to get the juices flowing. Stop frequently to get out and stretch while you walk around the RV and do a visual check. Consider a gym membership at a nationwide chain.

- Drive only as far as you are comfortable in a day and don't push yourself to exhaustion. With preplanning, you can space out your mileage and arrive safe and fresh at your destination.

- Find the humor in whatever crazy thing happens along the way.

- Accept that there are going to be events you cannot control. It is how you react that counts.

The Surprise Shower

Perhaps my all-time favorite memory of "one of those days" is the little incident with the toilet in our brand new Heartland Caliber trailer. After Arnie and I had practiced wandering in our small hybrid Jayco for two years, we were nearly ready to retire and launch our full-time journey. We knew that it was time to trade in Dinky Doo and step up in size. This little unit had been the perfect unit for us at the time, but we had outgrown it. Times change and given that we would be spending nearly six months at a time on the road at that point, it seemed prudent to trade for something that would allow more than one person to stand at the same time. So we said a fond goodbye to Dinky and with a grateful wave for the good times, we drove off with a thirty-three foot Heartland Caliber trailer that felt spacious indeed in comparison.

It is fun getting to know a new RV home and our new home sweet home had lots of nice amenities. We had chosen this one carefully after lots of research and an extensive search. The greater length would give us so much more living area and room to navigate dogs underfoot. It had ample room for a crate for the new puppy we were expecting and Cracker's birdcage fit ideally in a free corner with storage underneath. I loved the roomy double closet in the bedroom and kitchen pantry. And it had slides. We had stepped up in the world of RV living, but we also had a lot to learn about our new home.

Every unit has its peculiarities and it does take time to get familiar with how everything works. There was quite a bit more to think about because this new unit came with considerably more bells and whistles. There was a myriad of details to re-member; did we remember to plug in the voltage meter, is the pressure regulator hooked up, is the fridge switched over to gas, is there any gas in the tanks? Is everything out of the way of the slides, are the steps retracted, awning in?

The toilet incident happened as we were getting familiar with the Heartland on a trial run and it qualifies as one of our epic "one of those days." Just so that you have a proper visual, RV bath-rooms are quite tight quarters, often with overhead cabinets, nooks and crannies for storage and a foot pedal for flushing. This eventful day, we had pulled into our site and were setting up camp. I usually take care of the inside set up tasks while Arnie sets about unhitching, leveling and hooking up to water, electric and sewer outlets.

One of the new bells and whistles that this unit has is an inlet to pressure clean the black water tank. For camping novices, the black water tank is the one that holds the nasty stuff. We empty it as we depart each campground, so it is fresh when we arrive at the next one. But fresh is a relative word. There is always a bit of residue and that is why the manufacturer provides a pressure cleaning function. You hook a hose up, make sure to open the outside valve to the black water tank and flush until it runs clear. With the right equipment, it is quite a smooth and sanitary procedure despite what you might imagine.

This day, we had rolled in tired, hungry and road-weary on our Maiden Voyage in our new RV. I got things set up inside and started dinner while Arnie hooked up the utilities. After just a bit, I heard a peculiar gurgling sound, so I went to the rear of the trailer to investigate in the bathroom where the noise seemed to originate. It sounded almost like a motor with running water. What could it be? I called out to Arnie and asked him. He went to check on the mystery noise and soon I heard him banging about outside the rear of the trailer and the mystery noise stopped. He did not come in with an explanation, so I assumed that all was well and the problem was solved because the sound went away. Never assume.

I needed to empty some wastewater from the sink into the black water tank, so I went into the bathroom and with my foot, depressed the pedal that opens the value on the toilet to flush it. Instantly a fully pressurized volcanic jet of brown liquid burst forth from the open commode, shooting straight up into the air, hitting the bottom of the overhead cabinets and then dripping down the walls. I only had the value open for a split second before I reacted and removed my foot from the pedal, but it was time enough for the toilet, now known as Vesuvius, to send a shocking and smelly shower all over the bathroom.

It seems that Arnie had hooked the water up to the wrong inlet, pressurizing the closed black water tank. When I opened it suddenly, the pressure had to release somewhere and up and out was the only direction. That would be why there is a sticker on that connection that says, "Make sure that the black water tank is open before making this connection." But who reads these things? Clearly not us. I did not even know we had that connection until this fortunate discovery.

I will be eternally grateful that I was standing up erect while dumping something into that toilet rather than in a seated position at the time of the explosion. Or I could have been bending over it and received a face full too. As it was, the spew missed me completely. Not a drop on the lily-white blouse I was wearing at the time. Our bathroom was not so lucky and Lysol is now my very best friend. As with most incidents like this, it's funny now and the important thing is that no one got hurt.

Say a Little Prayer

There will be days like this, but I promise there will be many more that are full of wonder as you wander. When that odd day comes along that tries your patience, it helps to be reflective and mindful of how you react in certain situations. For instance, as Arnie will tell you, I am a confident driver but a nervous rider, especially when we are hauling our home on wheels. It stresses me out when the big rigs rush by us on the highway or someone with no understanding of what it takes to stop an RV at fifty-five miles an hour cuts us off in traffic. I know this stresses me, so I do try very hard not to be over-reactive to these things that are out of my control. I also pray a lot.

Whatever your faith-base, prayer can be a powerful offset to tough times. It's a chance to begin again, to ask our dreams of the universe and to connect with something greater and wiser than ourselves with gratitude for where we are right now. So if you are driving down the road and you pass by our truck, you may see me in the front seat with my eyes squeezed shut. I am praying that we avoid a crash and grateful that we have not had one yet. Yes, Mama, there will be days like this that require prayers for safety. But there will be many more that go well and call for prayers of gratitude. Pray for more of those.

Chapter Thirteen
The Right Fit

"Late in the evening, tired and happy and miles from home, they drew upon a remote common far from habitations, turned the horse loose to graze, and ate their simple supper sitting on the grass by the side of the cart...[The] stars grew fuller and larger all around them, and a yellow moon, appearing suddenly and silently from nowhere in particular."
- Kenneth Grahame, The Wind in the Willows

If you have gotten this far into this book, I am going to assume that you are now serious about crafting a new life in an RV and that you are ready to go out and look for just the right fit. There is plenty of specific information available to you regarding what models and styles are available. But first, ask yourself what you want to do with your unit. Ask this before you begin thinking about specific models or forming opinions on preferred manufacturers. You are not buying this home to own it; you are buying it to go places and do things in it. Your chosen unit must have the capability to travel where you want and function under the conditions you prefer. You will need a broad focus at this stage of selecting an RV to achieve your travel goals. During your search, keep this broad focus.

Finding just the right accommodations for your journey will make the adjustment to life on the road easier and the hunt for exactly the right unit is fun. The time you spend attending RV shows and going to dealerships constitutes valuable research and it will pay off in the long run. You will be a better-informed buyer and more likely to choose something that fits your needs based on practicality rather than impulse.

Keeping this focus in mind, here are some initial questions that will help you in your search. As you look around, you will add more considerations and adapt this list as your own.

- What type of camping are you planning? Will you stay primarily in parks, or would you like to do some boondocking? Consider the off-road capability of any RV that interests you. Can it get out there and can it stay there for the length of time you are planning? Conversely, can you park it in a more urban setting?

- What size RV do you need? Small is easy to park and tight to live in. Large is tight to park and easy to live in. Find your comfort point.

- How many people are traveling with you? What are their special needs?

- Who will be doing the driving? Do you have a back-up driver? Are you both comfortable that you can handle the unit? Do some test drives.

- For our purposes here, we are talking about full-time or nearly full-time on the road. What compromises will this unit ask you to make? (i.e., foldable beds, limited storage, tiny shower)

- Will the unit you are considering need to handle cold and hot weather extremes?

- What is the storage capacity and does it fit your own unique needs? (i.e., dog kennels and fence, kayaks, bikes, grills, hobby supplies, work equipment and supplies)

- If you are towing, what is the towing capacity of your tow vehicle? Can it manage the terrain you intend to cover? Can it pull a fully loaded RV without stressing the engine? The choice of the tow vehicle is a critical consideration and not a detail that you can figure out after the fact.

- What are your non-negotiables? Do you have to have slides, a bunk room and a pantry? You can change colors, but not infrastructure, so think about the big picture at this stage.

- What is your budget? Find it, set it and stay within it. There is no point in owning that shiny new luxury RV if you cannot afford the gas to journey about in it.

After you develop and explore your list of broad questions, you can then move to the ideal specifics that you want in a unit. There will be compromises, but be sure they are ones that you are willing to make without unnecessary irritation. This travel experience is uniquely your own and these preliminary types of questions are a reality check to keep you grounded as you pursue your dream. So give yourself the time to ask the hard questions, tally up your answers and use it as a checklist for shopping for your new home. Soon it will be parked in your driveway and you will be getting to know one another.

All That Glitters

There is one mistake that is commonly made by folks who are new to the traveling life. Be careful not to overbuy on your first purchase. Going to the RV Dealership and browsing among all of the shiny new models is so much fun and it is one of our favorite weekend pastimes. But this Sunday afternoon activity can result in impulsive buyers who have not adequately done their homework, buying more than they can handle. Bigger is not always better. One piece of advice that we frequently offer is to start smaller and trade your way up gradually to a size that you are comfortable handling on the road and living in. It is no fun to be anxious in a rig that is just too much to handle with confidence or one that stretches finances so far that buying gas is out of reach on the monthly budget. Ease into this commitment with prudence and common sense so that you can sustain your passion for wandering for the long run. An experienced salesperson should understand this and assist you in choosing a rig that meets not only your wish list but also your skill level and your experience level too.

It is so easy to become enamored with some of the beautiful models available today. With their glittering granite counters, big-screen TVs, surround sound DVD players and other luxurious amenities, they offer an almost irresistible appeal to folks longing for a comfortable escape into nature. It is easy to fall hard and fast. Camping expos fill with people dreaming of an escape on wheels. Touring the country in a traveling getaway home is enticing and the very thought of it can cause sane people to go all starry-eyed. They wander longingly among the mammoth rigs fully equipped for interplanetary travel. I once asked a dealer, "Who can afford these things?" He chuckled and responded, "No one. But that does not stop anyone from falling in love with them." He went on to explain that a vast majority of the big coaches come back into the dealership for resale within six months when the bloom is off the rose and the new owners realize what driving one entails.

One issue that new owners often do not anticipate is the fact that the very large rigs will have some limits on where they can go. State and national parks are notoriously tricky to camp in if your RV is too long. You will need to take into consideration the combined lengths of the tow vehicle and the trailer/fifth wheel or the motorhome and the towed vehicle when deciding if you can fit into any available site. Some parks have only a few spots that will accommodate larger units and those sites go quickly. A good example is Acadia National Park's Blackwoods Campground. They can only accommodate thirty-five feet in combined length and the slide outs must fit in the space too. So, if you have a toad (a car you are towing behind the motorhome), then you really would not be able to get in with anything much longer than 29 feet for the RV itself to fit the letter of the law. Ask yourself what style of travel unit fits your particular goals? Make sure that you chose the right rig that will be capable of transporting you to the places you are longing to see.

But there will be many privately owned parks that provide the courtesy of well-designed pull-through sites to reduce the aggravation of trying to skinny that RV in between two trees and a boulder. These accommodations may be more your style. I always say that pull-through sites are suitable for marriages that have a low tolerance for stress. The rest of the parks are designed by some engineering masochist who enjoys the spectacle of seeing us trying to line up forty-foot rigs with the picnic table, the fire ring and the water/sewer hookups.

Learning the Ropes

When you do find just the right rig for you, you will begin your learning curve on how to operate it. Dealerships offer some outstanding workshops to help you with getting oriented to your new home on wheels. It takes some practice to develop the skill to pull and back an RV, especially a towable trailer if you have never done it before. It is not intuitive. I would highly recommend attending some of the great workshops offered by dealers and at RV Expos to learn all that you can before departing. YouTube also has many instructional videos posted to help the novice. But I contend that watching a video or reading about how to back up a trailer is one thing. Sitting in the seat and attempting the feat is quite another, put in your practice time.

Arnie and I have had this talk more than once. Backing up the trailer is not exactly his forte, but researching it is. In fact, in terms of studying the subject, he is the Stephen Hawking of RVs, the theory of all things trailer. That is my husband, hunched over the computer doing an excellent job of research on the physics of correctly backing up a rig according to a variety of experts. He has collected data from all sources and probably could write a manual on the subject. But doing it is another thing. I say this with no snark; Arnie can't back up the trailer.

Luckily, Arnie has a secret weapon to help with backing up. Me. He handles the drive forward and I do the backing up. It is one of the separations of duties that I mentioned before; each person contributes according to their skillset. His nickname for me is Large Marge and I wear the moniker proudly. Remember Alice Nunn, the slightly disturbed truck driver from *Pee Wee's Big Adventure*? [1] I have that same red flannel shirt she wore in Tim Burton's classic film and I can put that rig into a pencil-thin spot between two leaning trees. My preternatural backing skill is a bonus to our marriage to be sure, as I keep reminding him.

Parking is camping foreplay. You have to do it before the real fun begins. Sometimes it goes well and, well, sometimes it just doesn't. But we admit that it is perverse entertainment to watch couples park the trailer together. On one particularly hot afternoon, we arrived at our campsite after a long day of driving. As usual, Arnie hopped out of the cab to offer direction and I slid over into the driver's seat to do the dirty work. There was a woman with a toddler on a three-wheeler watching from the roadside and I heard her caution the little boy. "Stay here, Bubba. That's a woman backing up."

I refrained from responding due to the need to concentrate on the ridiculously tight space the park had assigned to us.

Barb: "Okay?"

Arnie: "Okay. Okay."

Barb: "Okay, here we go."

Arnie: "Okay. No. No, turn your wheels."

Barb: "Which way?"

Arnie: "That way? Right."

Barb, patiently: "Which right, yours or mine?"

Arnie, who has now stepped out of sight: "Mine, that way. No the other way. The other way! My way."

Barb, patiently: "I can't see you."

Arnie, stepping back into sight: "You're holding up traffic. Back up."

Barb, patiently: "They will have to wait. I can't hurry this. Okay?"

Arnie; Okay. "Just back up. Now stop. Stop, stop STOP! Why didn't you stop?"

Barb, testily: "Were you talking? I couldn't hear you 40 feet behind me with the engine running."

Arnie, making some vague, unknown hand signal: "When I motion like this STOP."

Barb, entirely over it: "I thought you were swatting flies. I'll pull out and start again."

There is a moral of the story. While RV shows might offer some real deals, nothing is a good deal if you are uncomfortable driving it, backing it up, parking it or setting it up. At this point early in our travels, we lacked some agreed-upon signals along with not having any auxiliary equipment to help us out. If we had already taken a class we would have understood how to use hand signals between us more effectively. Another solution is a back-up camera where I would be able to see Arnie at any point in his wild hand gestures. A two-way radio or headset system between us so that we could talk to each other without shouting over the engine noise would have been helpful too. These are simple solutions that can make life much easier.

Make sure you can work together to manage whatever rig you chose. Under-buy rather than over-buy, do your research on every trade carefully and take one step at a time. Never shop when wanderlust is clouding your judgment. This practice has kept us comfortable in our mobile spaces and confident when we are on the move.

Backing up is not the only challenge. It is vital to get the right fit in both directions. Let's talk about driving forward, pulling the trailer down the road with the truck. It's all good when you strike out from home for a fun weekend and see that long stretch of road ahead of you. Who could imagine the obstacles that could pop up; roadblocks, detours, low overhangs, road construction with potholes, quick lane changes and the list goes on. My pet peeve is the truckers who pull up alongside you on the highway at top speed and blow their ear-splitting air horn at you for some unknown road transgression. That would be the air horn that gives you cardiac arrest when it lifts you right out of your seat on the highway. Just the startle effect from that horn could cause a pile-up. Angels have mercy on you if you come anywhere near their personal space, which is racing down the road at 70 MPH. Not to mention that for a brief moment in time, he was driving that monster one-handed as he gave you the single-digit salute.

But we have to drive somewhere to get somewhere. Having equipment that is the right fit for us keeps us and everyone else on the road safer and more secure. Despite all proper preparations, there will always be those unexpected events along the way and we might as well lose any notion that all will come off perfectly. Despite all of our careful planning, RV living will challenge us with plenty of unexpected potholes in the open road. Choose carefully and be sure that you end up with traveling equipment that suits your wants, as well as your skillset. Be very realistic about what you can handle and try it out first.

After you choose your unit, you can turn your attention to the fun stuff. There is a whole continuum of choices of gear and accessories to enhance our RVing experience. Establishing your home on wheels is not only exciting, but it can be a spiritual endeavor. It is essential to have fun picking out just the right unit for your travels, but also just as necessary to outfit your space with sensitivity. It does not need to cost a fortune, but this is the environment where you will be living a new and very different life. It deserves to be a well thought out space with practical equipment that enhances your experience. Home is not bricks and mortar, nor is it fiberglass or steel, but rather, an emotional state. Your feelings of belonging, family, security and memories are a balm to anxiety and longing. Bring along a few precious items to make it your new "Home Sweet Home." And be sure to leave room for a few treasures along the way.

One thing that every wanderer has in common is a fascination with camping equipment, commonly known as gear. It is one collective obsession that binds all of us road nuts together in a like-minded community. Whether you plan to get outdoors in a tent, a small RV unit, or travel the road in a big rig with luxury amenities, you will find yourself talking about gear with other wanders frequently. If you need an icebreaker to start up a conversation with another traveler, throw out a compliment on some piece of equipment at their site. It is a great way to meet people and find common ground. We all are interested in comparing notes on everything from the tow vehicle and the RV itself to our favorite gadgets, tools, backpacks, binoculars, etc. Wanderers can talk gear all day and all night and it is the context of many conversations around shared fires. Everyone who travels has a story about choosing the right or the wrong gear. I love to tell the story of Big Blue.

I am a gear head. I don't read People or Cosmopolitan magazine, but I do pour over the LL Bean catalog. I can skip Macy's, but I love to visit Bass Pro Shops. Like many campers, I have a frugal streak and I appreciate a bargain, so I visit thrift shops often. I justify it by saying being thrifty is a necessity not a choice in retirement but the truth is, I enjoy thrift shopping, especially for camping gear and equipment. I have added sets of sheets and towels that would not have made sense to purchase at full price. Stacking plastic organizers, drawer dividers and lightweight casserole dishes were all fortunate finds at the Salvation Army thrift store. And the cozy plaid flannel shirts found at a Value Village are comforting on cold nights in front of the fire. But the very best score was many seasons ago when I found a fabulous piece of camping gear in an unlikely place.

My friend Penny and I were scouting out the local Goodwill store and I spied the prize on an end aisle. Be still my heart. It was a pop-up screen room that was brand new, still in the box and a beautiful shade of bright blue. The box claimed it was 6 x 6 and roomy enough for four people. The description bragged, "Just pops up right into place," The package described it as, "easy to fold and comes with its own compact carrying bag." My eyes glazed over like most women do when they find that perfect pair of shoes. I was in shopping heaven for nature lovers. I could not get it to the cash register fast enough. Penny and I raced home with the anticipation of trying out how it "pops up right into place." I was eager to see my purchase spring to life in all of its big blue glory.

That Saturday was a sweltering Florida day, so Penny and I decided to take Big Blue into the living room where we could check it out in air-conditioned comfort. We broke into the box and pulled out a tightly wound, spring-loaded circle in a nice carrying bag. It was folded up exactly like the silver reflective sunblock screen that fits in your car's windshield. The principle of the spring was the same. It is designed to be easy, neat and compact. Penny prepared to read the directions while I just dove in with my usual reckless disregard for written instructions. After all, the box says, "Pops upright into place." Lo and behold, it does just that.

Who knew it was 6 x 6 and SIX FEET TALL TOO. In a millisecond, the beast burst the confines of the tight fold that kept it in the bag, vaulted to full size in my living room and took a right good beating from the ceiling fan. While Penny dissolved laughing on the couch, I dragged poor Big Blue away from the pummeling it was getting from the fan. In typical fashion, I had moved right on past the fact that the box clearly said, "Caution, never open in a closed area."

Now, with the oversized monster open and moved to relative safety, we began virtual decorating. We imagined where we would place the camp chair, how well the small table would fit and exactly where the cooler with the Coronas would go. We imagined how well the zippered door would keep those pesky mosquitoes in their proper place: outside. When those decor details were decided upon, we realized it was now time to face another challenge. Now we must put Big Blue back in the little tiny bag. Remember how hard it is to fold up that windshield screen the first time? Make it a screen house and you can imagine the antics of the next half hour trying to coax that screen house back into the bag.

This time, having learned a valuable lesson from the thumping my new toy just took, I read the directions. Penny offered to help, but I declined. I reminded her that I must be able to manage this problem because I camp alone (this was pre-Arnie). I must master this solitary task like the able solo camper I am. The directions are specific: Walk one corner into the opposite corner, fold it like a book, flip it upside down, bring the bottom edge down to meet the top side, stand on the rim with both feet to stabilize it and lower it into an arc down to thigh level. Next, cross your wrists and push the corner into the center and it will collapse easily onto itself. Well, trust me, it is not that simple.

What happened next was the equivalent of an audition for a contortionist in the circus. I teetered and balanced, wrestled with it and laid on it, swore at it and it still sprang back up "right in place." Every time I got it nearly compact enough to stuff neatly into the bag, it erupted to life again with a vengeance. With maniacal intent, Big Blue aimed at me. It meant to harm and humiliate me and I was taking the beating personally. An evil life force possessed my happy thrift store find.

After a humbling period of struggle, I did eventually manage to wrestle Big Blue into submission. I think I even learned a few valuable lessons about the importance of doing prudent research before taking impulsive action, accepting help from others and slowing down to think through problems rather than just muscling through them. These were all suitable lessons to prepare me for a full-time life on the road as I would encounter many similar situations in the future. When faced with a decision or problem involving equipment on the road now, I often remind myself to channel Big Blue for a better outcome.

I went on to camp harmoniously with Big Blue for many seasons and finally mastered the technique of coaxing it in and out of its bag without incurring a black eye each time. Sadly, one year at the onset of camping season, when I went to check the camping gear for wear and tear, I found that Blue's lifespan had reached its limit. The heat and sun had rotted seams and Blue was no longer usable. I felt a certain sadness saying goodbye to my old foe. I had hand-painted the likenesses of my two dogs and my parrot Cracker on its sides, so Big Blue had been my conversation starter for many years and an excellent equipment fit. I set up Crackers traveling cage inside to keep him safe from insects and crawly things and the dogs enjoyed the freedom of a larger enclosure versus a crate.

When you have equipment that is a good fit for you, you will enjoy a more relaxed journey and be freer to enjoy seeing wild ponies, taking swamp hikes, listening to mountain music and visiting fall festivals. Let your well-fit unit and proper equipment facilitate conversation and connection with fellow wanderers and bring you deeper into community.

[1] https://www.youtube.com/watch?v=lPMSGTfK4Aw

Chapter Fourteen
Two by Two: Pets Aboard

"Parrots make great pets. They have more personality than goldfish."
- Chevy Chase

Just as the animals boarded the ark two by two, all sorts of pets are boarding RVs to travel with their owners. Dogs and cats are the most common traveling companions and the joy that they bring to their owners is undeniable. In addition to dogs and cats, people are now traveling with a surprising array of other species as companions, including hamsters, fish, rats, guinea pigs, snakes, sugar gliders, iguanas, ferrets, chinchillas and the occasional pot-bellied pig.

No matter what species shares your space, some adjustments will undoubtedly be required. Traveling pets have been taken out of their familiar environment too and have to get used to strange spaces and new routines. Many of these more exotic animals need specialized equipment, diets and habitats that will take up space, time and money on your trips. You will have to give thought to how you will handle their individual needs. Special diets, access to proper exercise and medications are considerations and if separation anxiety is an issue, allocating precious space for a crate may be necessary. Asking yourself how you will accommodate your pets as part of your road family is part of the process of careful planning for your upcoming wandering life. Just as you have given lots of thought to how you will make the transition to RVing, you will need to consider how your animal companions will fare.

Our own experience with blending our furry and feathered family offered us some valuable insights. Arnie and I were in the same high school class and connected again quite by chance when we were in our early sixties. As we grew closer and considered making a new life together, we had a bit of a dilemma. At the time, I lived with Hana and Wicca, two little dogs and Cracker, a fussy old African Grey parrot. Arnie roomed with Leo, a huge orange bachelor cat, an only child who hadn't met many other people. We were unsure how we would combine all of the stepchildren and be fair to everyone. Our commitment to our animals was uncompromising and we did not want to sacrifice anyone's safety or comfort. We had to figure out how to live together in harmony, first in a shared homeland ultimately in an RV.

There are various ways to introduce animals to one another. Of course, the safety of everyone concerned is paramount and you will need to carefully evaluate the best course of action when introducing your pets to sharing a small confined space. While it may not be appropriate for everyone, we decided to take the most direct route, putting everyone in the same place together under close supervision so that they could sort it out amongst themselves. We, of course, used precautions but it worked out quite smoothly. You may need to go slower and safer with your own pets.

We were most concerned about combining the cat and the bird as they are not natural co-habitants. But our fears were unfounded. Although Leo had been a feral cat who had been forced to scrap and fight for the first part of his life, he walked through the door and took command of the whole household with a very Buddha-nature. Leo never gave a second glance to Cracker, but rather set the tone for tolerance and acceptance from the first moment in his new house with his new family members. The eighteen-pound gentle giant padded in, not with bully arrogance, but with curiosity and zest for exploring these new relationships. His calm manner established a balance of

166

equals and he seemed to know just how to behave to be in the right relationship with each individual. He adjusted his demeanor to make everyone comfortable with his presence even though he was the biggest guy on the block and they were all there first.

As an added perk, Leo fell head over heels in love with Hana, appearing not to understand that he was a cat and she was a princess. He never gave up trying to win her affection. Leo loved to lay next to Hana, tapping her gently on the rump with his soft velvet paw. Feline feet pounded down the hallway as he chased her joyfully. Despite her typical Japanese Chin aloofness, it was enough for him to get up each day and see that she was there. He generously asked little from Hana other than to be close to her.

Leo sadly and suddenly passed away two weeks before we started our traveling life and we miss him still. With his accepting nature, we think he would have been a great wandering companion. We learned three lessons from Leo and we like to apply his cat wisdom to our life on the road.

Lesson One: Leo moved past his history and right into the present moment, adapting quickly to his new normal. He taught the lesson that baggage from the past doesn't need to define our lives going forward. Staying grounded in the present is something to strive for as we leave behind our material baggage and conventional norms to embark on a new mobile life.

Lesson Two: Leo modeled how to be a peaceful participant in his daily life and each of the other animals followed his example. Despite the co-living challenges, he chose never to be cross at anyone and always to be willing to step aside. Life on the road can bring us into some close quarters and shared facilities. It goes easier when we adopt an attitude of other-mindedness and generosity towards our fellow travelers.

Lesson Three: Leo loved Hana. If karma follows intention, he intended only to be in a loving relationship with her, the one he revered the most. She was not always gracious back, especially around the dinner bowl. He taught us that when the inevitable tensions arise, don't fight over the food dish.

Cats, dogs, birds, rabbits, guinea pigs- all animals have the capacity to adapt to their surroundings if you give them the time and support to do so. And the best news is that they are natural ambassadors who will draw you into conversation with other people in a relaxed natural way.

One year we took a trip down to Marathon Key, halfway down the Florida Keys to attend Hawkfest, a large bird watching event. It was the first time we attended this event and we did not know anyone. By the end of the week, thanks to Cracker, we would know everyone- or at least, they would know us.

We were assigned a handy site right below the platform where a group of the researchers and their volunteer students were counting migrating hawks, falcons and songbirds. Their task was to identify various species stopping over on their migration route and compare the numbers to years past. What they did not know is that Cracker instantly picks up whatever birds' voices are in the vicinity of where he is camping. He delights in confusing the native species by calling to them. The wild birds fly down looking for love, check him out and leave embarrassed at being fooled.

The researchers found themselves fooled too. They were responsible for identifying the wild calls of hawks and songbirds and they had to be careful not to count Crackers expert imitations. But they were good sports and amused by Cracker's endless stream of bird calls, whistles and words that he's picked up along the way. He called "Peek-a-boo, I see you." to the volunteer counters and punctuated the quiet campground with an occasional, "Hot Damn!" Each morning when they arrived, they would greet him with "Good morning, Cracker." "I love you." he'd reply.

We have encountered many people who are fascinated with birds and take them along as traveling companions. Cracker has been a great way to meet people who are curious about him, especially children. However, we do try to help everyone we meet understand more about the pros and cons of acquiring any parrot as a pet; they are messy, loud and expensive to feed. Birds like Cracker are either captive bred or caught in the wild. In either case, life in a cage is unnatural and not in any way ideal. If you love birds and are considering traveling with one, contact a bird rescue group to learn how you can adopt an abused or neglected bird in need of a new home. Please don't add to the suffering by purchasing a bird from a pet store.

Cracker came to us quite by chance and not by choice, but we are his guardians for this lifetime, responsible for his well-being in captivity. Because he cannot fly free, we owe him the kindest and most compassionate circumstances that we can provide. Thus, his safety and comfort were considerations when we looked for an RV that would be the right fit. We consider him a beloved friend and companion and we respect his intelligence and his willingness to adapt to our moving about in different environments. He's the equivalent of a crazy uncle who's along for the ride.

Gearing Up for Pets

It requires a fair amount of gear to make pets comfortable and safe while traveling. You don't want to cart along too much, but certain pieces of equipment will make your life on the road with animals easier. It is a pet peeve for many when they find themselves parked adjacent to a site, whose dog is making a sonic assault on the campground, barking incessantly. While bark collars are controversial, out of consideration for others, it may be necessary gear to consider if your dog is a chronic barker. If you object to using a bark collar, then invest in training before you go. The American Kennel Club website offers useful information on their Canine Good Citizen [1] certification and I highly recommend getting this training for your traveling dog. Some campgrounds are beginning to require it.

One essential piece of equipment that we keep on board and use is a doggie gate. It comes in handy when we need to separate the dogs and also when we have company. On one eventful night, one of the dogs was having a medical issue and we didn't want her roaming loose at night and having an accident. It seemed like a good idea to confine her in the bedroom with us so that she could alert us if she needed to go out. The last thing I said before going to bed that night was, "Let's not get up and forget that gate is there." Those were prophetic words. It wasn't ten minutes before Arnie decided he had better get out of bed and double-check the front door to be sure he locked it for the night. You can't be too careful, you know.

Hopping out of bed and striding right along, he hit the gate first with his right foot, jamming his big toe into one of the lattice squares. The crash was chilling. Launched forward, he then hit the floor and flipped over on his back, in the process, firmly planting the other big toe in the lattice also. There he was, flipped on his back, feet in the air, with a dog gate stuck on his toes.

From this position of grace, he proceeded to moan loudly, "My toes, my toes, my toes! Pull the gate off my toes." I did a speed jump out of bed, ran to his assistance and tried to help. But toes are pretty crooked little things. Once wedged into a small space, they don't just slip out again easily. I had to carefully jiggle that gate gently back and forth to release those two snug little buggers from their trap. But the tight fit was not nearly the biggest obstacle to this catch and release effort.

The biggest obstacle was how hard I was laughing. The sight of my unfortunate husband flat on his back and balancing a dog gate on his two big toes, all the while pleading for relief overcame me. It's a character flaw, I know, but I can't help but laugh when something like this happens. I try, but it overtakes my self-control. It's like some involuntary sort of hysteria that overrides my compassion and good sense. Now, don't get me wrong, I did rush to his assistance and I did extricate Arnie from his predicament quite quickly. I do feel a little bit wrong about the laughing, but God help me, every time I picture this, I laugh all over again.

Thunderstruck

Thunderstorms are a special consideration as they strike terror in the heart of many dogs and can cause acute anxiety. A fearful dog left alone in an RV during a storm can do extensive damage in a short time trying to escape or hide. Dogs are safest when they are leashed or contained during storms so that there is no chance of them getting separated and lost. We've heard some sad stories from other travelers about losing a precious pet during a storm and having to move on without finding them. You can avoid this heartbreak with careful planning and provision of the right equipment plus keeping an eye on the weather forecast.

Our Hana is not an enthusiastic traveler but she is an excellent forecaster. There are challenges for the princess wherever we go and one of the most significant challenges is the weather. Weather can be unpredictable anywhere. As any new storm approaches in the distance, Hana's anxiety rises. All we can do is abide with her, sad that she must undergo the fear and frustration of uncontrollable events. She only understands the anxiety of the moment and cannot anticipate the redemptive power of surrendering to the ebb and flow of life. She only knows that the storm will come and doesn't understand that it will also go.

It starts subtly. Far away across the mountain, a rumble begins to form that is undetectable to human ears. A storm begins to brew in the distance and our first warning sign is the unease of this small dog. Hana alerts us of the coming weather before we even know it is coming. As the wind begins to gust and howl and the rain drums on the roof, her slight anxiety swells into a state of fright that is distressing to watch. The storm is a parable for life's way of throwing unexpected and unwelcome events our way. It has not only snatched away the promise of a quiet afternoon of lying outside, but it has invaded this little one's life with palpable peril. Hana finds refuge where she can, huddled in a corner, curled into a ball in a favorite bed or pacing the floor endlessly while the wind howls and bays.

After it subsides, she's exhausted and falls into a deep sleep for a time. When the sunshine finally peeks through again, she forgives the rain quickly and continues with her doggie plans for the day. Within minutes, Hana is barking at the chipmunks and watching for the dog walkers who she feels are encroaching on her territory.

Even life's stormiest spells eventually come to pass. Although we can't will them away, we can surrender to the belief that the unclouded blue skies will return. The rain surely helps us to appreciate the sun. Maybe we need the dark days to appreciate the light? Meanwhile, we are just grateful that Hana's quiet and happy again.

A Perfect Match

Encounters with people and their pets can often be inspiring. It can also teach us to put our assumptions aside. One beautiful Virginia day we pulled into one of our favorite spots nestled between a rolling hill with flocks of sheep and a cow pasture. We love watching the farmer and his border collie rotate the flock with the herd each afternoon, expertly changing their pastures. The dog is poetry in motion as he does his work. He responds to the farmer's whistles as he zigs and zags herding all of the animals to the exact right spot through the gate.

On this visit, we happened to camp beside an elderly lady, Doris, who was traveling alone. She was driving a medium-sized Class C Coach that would be a challenge for anyone to negotiate in many situations, but she handled it like a pro. Imagine our surprise when she came out of her Class C with a huge, muscled Doberman. Bailey is the kind of dog that you might think would require a very physically able and assertive owner, someone with the strength to keep him behaving properly in close campground quarters. But Doris was frail and unsteady on her feet. It was a challenge for her to step down her stairs and walk to sit at the picnic table. At first glance, it seemed like a puzzling match and we looked at one another with concern. Being a die-hard dog lover, I just had to go over and admire this handsome animal and ask Doris if she needed any assistance.

She shared that she's a retired Licensed AKC Judge of Dobermans and several other working and herding breeds and was coming home from a show. Becoming an AKC judge is no easy accomplishment. It requires years of experience, training and study. She was a contemporary of many of the people who I grew up with and knew in the dog show world when I was a young person showing and handling dogs myself. We had a wonderful time talking and reminiscing about growing up in the dog world and I was so pleased to meet her. It was clear that Bailey was the perfect dog for her. He moved carefully around her, taking caution not to knock into her, maneuvering slowly to accommodate her unsteadiness. He sat quietly staring into her eyes as we talked, occasionally putting his massive head into her lap. Doris raised many dogs over the years. "With me being eighty and Baily being eight, this guy will most likely be my last dog." She shared that he gives her a sense of safety and companionship. "He's my boy."

Pets can help us to wander mindfully. The foundation of mindfulness includes attention, intention, compassion and awareness. These are all qualities inherent in the human/pet bond. While we humans have to learn these qualities and work on them, our pets practice them innately. We hope that you too may travel well with the precious companions of your choosing and those that choose you.

[1] https://www.akc.org/products-services/training-programs/canine-good-citizen/

Chapter Fifteen
Where the Road Ends

"However capable and skillful an individual may be, left alone, he or she will not survive. When we're sick or very young or very old, we must depend on the support of others. There is no significant division between us and other people because our basic natures are the same. If we wish to ensure everyone's peace and happiness we need to cultivate a healthy respect for the diversity of our peoples and cultures, founded on an understanding of this fundamental sameness of all human beings."
- The 14th Dalai Lama

This book has been mostly about taking you on a journey of self-discovery as you plan for your RVing adventure. I have given you some thoughtful questions to consider and some highlights from the experiences and journeys of others who have made the same transition that you're considering. Here is a bottom-line truth: we know from the whole of our life paths that the future of each life experience is its disappearance. Since we wanderers are transients ourselves, we know well that all things in life are transient. Our wilderness souls have destined us to a life of travel, so we accept that the destiny of every experience in that life is impermanence.

Through travel, we deepen our connection with the natural world. We stop along the way and see the stream running by on its way to the sea, smell the sweet grass and feel the wind steal our breath. Transience makes a ghost out of each experience. There was never a sunrise that didn't blend gently into noon, never a noon which didn't burn itself into fading nightfall and never a dusk that didn't give in to the dark cover of night. All things are impermanent, all seasons recede into silent memory and this nomadic time too shall pass.

In interviews, I have heard from young families that they were encouraged forward by the knowledge that their time with young children won't last forever. They want to go on epic trips together and see the wonder through their children's eyes. When I had a big family of young children, it would have been hard for me to imagine another life outside of hearth and home and responsibility. But today's young families are so wise. They understand that birds flock in the sky, making patterns of flight in the air and then they disappear.

And so it is with older travelers too. When we gather at the fire, a common theme among camping folk is, "We wanted to travel while we were able." We hear this phrase over and over and we certainly can relate personally to it. We often talk with aging wanderers who find that there is a turning point in their journey where they recognize the need to be near family once again. Perhaps they are not as confident driving anymore. Or, maybe they tire more quickly and easily. The continuity of regular medical care providers may be necessary. Some folks scale back to part-time, settling in near adult children and taking shorter trips. Some travel seasonally to milder weather in the winter and stay put in the summer. This gradual easing back helps them acclimate to a new living arrangement and a more traditional community. There are practical considerations that convince some wanders that it is time to curtail their journeys.

One couple that I met and interviewed, Merle and Marybeth, traveled full-time for eighteen and a half years. Now they have scaled back to part-time. They venture down from Minnesota to Arizona each winter in their fifth wheel. In the summer, they return to a cozy in-law apartment that their son and his wife fixed up for them in their home near Philadelphia. Marybeth says that she's grateful for the generosity that the kids have shown. "I appreciate what the kids have done for us and I understand that they'd like us to stay put now. But I'm only seventy and Merle is seventy-four. We're healthy and not ready to completely give up our trailer yet. We meet friends at a place in Arizona that we like every winter and we'd be very unhappy with a cold winter up north."

Merle thinks that he will know when the time is right. "We stop when we know we need to stop. We aren't foolish about it. We drive shorter days now and we stop for longer intervals. But, the time hasn't come yet to quit altogether. We still have a lot to see and places to be. We know there's a home to go to when we're ready."

Merle and Marybeth are fortunate to have a family waiting in the wings to help out when the time comes that they need it. Merle calls the apartment their granny flat. "That's because Granny enjoyed decorating it." Where it's possible and practical, this seems like an excellent solution to bridge the transition back to a home without wheels. In the Southwest, we have heard in-law suites called casitas and in Hawaii, ohana units. They provide some privacy and independence under the same roof and may also add to the value of the existing home.

One lady that we met was living in a variation of the same theme. When her home became too much to manage, her daughter and son-in-law moved into the house. She moved to the backyard where she converted a small barn into an in-law suite that is just right for her. She calls it her she-shed. She still loves camping and spends many summer weekends in her diminutive vintage trailer with a group of friends who are vintage trailer aficionados. Like Merle and Marybeth, she's found a way to have her cake and eat it too. They all are bridging the gap in practical ways that make sense for them.

Not everyone has such good options for bringing their RVing to a close. For many, the thought of leaving behind the wandering way of life is just simply unthinkable. They may have been mobile for an extended time, even years. There may be no family to return to and returning to their root community is no longer a good option. For some, there is no proper plan for the end of the road.

When we find ourselves where the road ends, we ask the very same question we began with- is the mobile lifestyle right for me? The answer was once yes, but someday, because all things change, the answer may be different. When being on the road is no longer working out well, then where does the mobile life logically conclude? How do we wind down a life of RVing and craft yet another transition? There must be a place over the last hill where folks could gather as a collection of nomads who are no longer able to be nomadic.

Maybe folks will evolve into some end of the trail living situation? Perhaps we will all be so reluctant to give up the wandering that we circle the wagons somewhere and support one another as we enter into the final season? There will undoubtedly be communities of aging RVers who no longer are willing or able to negotiate the roads. But they still may want or need to live in their beloved mobile spaces for as long as possible.

Finding a New Place to Call Home

Many full-timers are very happy with their RVs as a primary residence. They do not wish to go back to a land-based home, even though driving long distances is becoming harder for them. As the number of retirees adopting this lifestyle continues to expand, the needs of this alternative aging population will also grow. One popular travel club, Escapees RV Club, is addressing this very issue. Escapees CARE Center (Continuing Assistance for Retired Escapees) [1] is a 501(c)(3) nonprofit (tax-exempt) corporation formed in 1992 in recognition of the fact that there are circumstances in which full-time travelers need help. Sometimes, full-timers find that they are not able to take care of their own or their spouse's needs due to illness, injury, surgery or the progression of a long-term health situation. What then?

CARE's mission is to provide a haven in their campground, for members whose travels are curtailed because of age or temporarily interrupted because of health problems. Located in Livingston, Texas, CARE staffs *Rainbow's End* campground with professional assistance at affordable prices. Residents stay in their own RV units in a familiar friendly setting. They receive professional help with tasks of daily living that they may no longer be able to accomplish for themselves. Its goal is to delay or eliminate the need for a nursing home or assisted living. Staff and volunteers provide meals and transportation to medical appointments and have an adult day care center on the property.

Escapees CARE, Inc. provides its assisted living services at very affordable rates due to the generosity of Escapees RV Club members who help with monetary donations and volunteering. As the mobile population continues to grow, I believe that we will see the emergence of other creative solutions such as CARE to support people in place when they need assistance. We can only hope that in the future other organizations or government agencies will get involved and provide housing parks and necessary supports for folks who have their home on wheels but need a space to park it. This could provide a low-cost living alternative for seniors and others in need, at a fraction of the cost that it might require to build traditional housing units.

Parks that welcome campers who stay on-site, full-time are another viable solution for folks who are no longer able to move about full-time. In every state, there are over-55 parks that welcome those who wish to park their unit permanently in one location. In this choice of living arrangement, they can establish residency, access local services and age comfortably in place. They can still live in the smaller quarters that are familiar and work for them. It is not at all uncommon for natural supports to be provided between members of these communities by other seniors who help one another out when a helping hand is needed. Reciprocal relationships arise naturally within the group and enhance the quality and safety of life for everyone in it.

We met Sam and Carolyn in 2011. They had been traveling together for about ten years and had just recently decided to get married. At the time, they were in their late seventies and in the process of winding down their journeys. They had done a lot of research on what made sense next and they had chosen to buy a site in a 55+ park in Florida that was close to excellent health care. Sam had experienced a mild heart attack in 2010. Sam was looking forward to the many activities and amenities that the park provides. Best of all, they could stay living in their familiar home on wheels. "I'm probably just fine to continue driving the big rig, but I feel a responsibility to everyone else on the road. That heart attack came out of nowhere. What if I was behind the wheel and it happened again? I can't take that chance." Carolyn agreed. "I think it's just time for us to park the bus. We'd had a wonderful time on the road, but I was looking forward to spending more relaxed, quiet time without the work of packing up and moving about so much. I wanted to be a homebody again."

We checked in on Sam and Carolyn again in 2013 and found them loving their new living arrangements. At that time, Sam was playing golf regularly and had not had any further complications with his heart condition. "I play golf with the guys twice a week and I volunteer at the Clubhouse for activities. Sometimes I miss traveling, but this is a good compromise for us here. Everyone here has a history of being on the road and we get together and talk about where we've been and what we've seen. Everyone has a story."

Carolyn is still working on putting together scrapbooks of their trips from maps, brochures and photos that they took over the ten years that they were RVing. "I love looking back, but honestly, I love looking forward more. We've got great friends here. We've got so much in common because we all traveled extensively. You get a more open mindset when you're on the road, so our friends here are from all over and we love them all."

I knew from our previous conversations that Sam and Carolyn had strong ties to the mobile community. They had been trip leaders for a travel group and had an extensive network of friends all across the country. I asked them specifically about how it was to leave their mobile friends and settle into one place again. Sam spoke of the values that were instilled in him growing up. "I came from a Midwestern town and the values there were old and traditional. I found those same values again when we started to travel. These are things like helping your neighbor and not letting older people get isolated with nothing to look forward to. I think that these 55+ parks are doing the same thing. It is like a small town where people help each other. If our neighbor needs something, we know about it and do something about it." Listening to Sam and Carolyn, it is clear that this type of communal living can be an excellent option for RVers who need or want to take a logical next step.

Finding Home Where You Are

An opportunity for another insightful interview arose when we met Vicki and Norman. They were in California when he had his heart attack. Vicki shared the story. "We'd been sightseeing at a winery in Napa Valley all day and when we returned to camp, Norm didn't feel very well and went to lay down for a bit. I

found him when I went up to the bedroom to call him for dinner. He wasn't coherent and he was very clammy. I called 911
and within fifteen minutes Norm was in the ambulance. He was
taken to the local hospital and later transferred about seven
hours south to Loma Linda, where he underwent a triple by-
pass."

I asked if Norm had any history of heart problems or if this was
a complete surprise. Vicki was candid. "There had been some
warning signs off and on. When we set out to travel, we knew
there would be medical issues to solve at some point. We did it
anyway. Our thought was, whatever arises we'll solve it where we
are at the time. We hoped nothing bad would happen, but you
never know."

Norm was candid too. "I had reservations about going full-time
since I'm seventy-four and Vicki is sixty-nine. We're not spring
chickens. But what were we going to do, stay home and wait for
the sky to fall? That just isn't us. We'd raised a family and we
wanted to travel." Vicki indicated that they took some precautions before leaving. "We prepared as well as we could without a
crystal ball to see the future. We both had physicals and got the
okay from our primary doctor. We put in place all our legal
documents: power of attorney, wills, health care surrogate, etc.
We got the best insurance we could afford, went to the gym for
six months to get in better shape and then off we drove."

The heart attack happened three years into their journeying.
"Truth be told, it didn't even hold us up that long. But it did
completely change how we are RVing." I asked Norm to explain
further.

"When I had my heart attack, we were staying a few days in a
small family run campground in one of their ten transient sites.
The rest of the campground is mostly permanent sites occupied

by the same people who either come seasonally or stay full-time. This is a tight-knit little enclave of people and the primary interest is fishing the surrounding lakes. Everyone has a boat. Generally, the men go off fishing and the wives enjoy fast friendships with each other. At five' o'clock, Happy Hour happens on the dock and we eat meals together three or four times a week. The few transient campers that pass-through for a couple of nights could never know how special this place. They are not here long enough to be a part of it."

Vicki jumped in. "But Norm and I had to stay three months while he recuperated and had physical therapy. These people immediately just took us under their angel wings. While Norm was in the hospital, I never felt alone. Our daughter flew out when it happened and when she had to go back to work in a week, she knew her Dad and I would have support from the other residents. They couldn't do enough to help us out."

I asked her to share with me specifically how belonging to this group of people had changed their RVing experience. "Well, we quit being on the road full-time. Now we move around only half the year and then we come right back here for six months to gather with our mobile family. Norm goes for his annual check-up and we settle in for the winter with friends all around us. This is the real deal. It's five o'clock somewhere and we know where."

The collective caring and wisdom of their mobile group knew what Norm and Vicki needed and provided it. Residents walked and fed their two dogs during the long days when Norm was in the hospital and Vicki stayed with him. The men did repairs on their unit, the women provided meals and everyone lent a listening ear when needed. Most of all, people gave Norm and Vicki a healing sense of belonging and their faraway children a welcome sense of relief that their parents were among friends.

183

These compassionate actions represent the RVing collective at its best.

In 2019, Arnie and I ended our full time wandering rather unexpectedly. Pressing family responsibilities and the fact that Arnie urgently needed a hip replacement converged and we made the tough decision to park the RV and move into a house once again. We needed to plan for the not too distant time when my mother would need more help and would need to come to live with us. So we settled on Georgia as the most logical location with its moderate climate and proximity to family. Each morning when we sit out on the deck to have coffee, we gaze over at the trailer. It is parked in its spot across the creek and we think about the time when we will load up and head out again. The wanderlust still whispers. The community still calls.

Has it ever been better put than by this excerpt from Kenneth Grahame's *Wind in the Willows*?

> *"Take the Adventure, heed the call, now ere the irrevocable moment passes!" 'Tis but a banging of the door behind you, a blithesome step forward and you're out of the old life and into the new! Then someday, some day long hence, jog home here if you will, when the cup has been drained and the play has been played and sit down by your quiet river with a store of goodly memories for company."*

Arnie and I do believe that we will begin our wandering again soon enough. We are, by our very nature, wanderers who need to share an allegorical fire and we know that it is in the miracle of connection to our mobile friends that all of our transfiguring journeys will live on. As humans struck by the wanderlust, we need a continuing link to nature and other like-minded souls who revel in it.

But for the moment, we are blooming where we are planted and addressing the practical considerations that have presented themselves. We will keep busy renovating the house while reminding ourselves not to get too attached, for this time of life also is impermanent. It won't be long before we meet you out there somewhere along the open road. We are very much looking forward to hearing your story.

Meanwhile, we hope that you all travel safe and well, embraced in the community of those who wander.

[1] https://www.escapees.com/benefits/rv-parking/escapees-rainbow-parks/livingston-tx/

Dedication

To my dad, Ed Wentzell, who built a square wooden camper on a metal chassis when I was a small child. He named it Bold Journey, painted it red, loaded up his fishing poles, boots and beer and set out on a fishing trip with his best friend Larry, leaving me sobbing in the driveway. The image of the fading tail lights on that red box of imaginative escape never left me. I vowed never to be left behind on an adventure again. Thanks, Dad, for the encouragement to think outside the box and never care what anyone said girls should or should not do. You encouraged my own Bold Journey.

This work is also dedicated to the life and spirit of Malia Lane whose life, travels and writings continue to inspire others to have the courage to follow their dreams.

Acknowledgements

This book was born in community, and if not for the grace of many people, it would never have come together. I'm indebted to the works of John Muir, Walt Whitman, and the life and wisdom of his holiness the Dalai Lama. The Tao Te Ching and the Bhagavad Gita are two sacred texts that framed the thought process for this book. These great thinkers have informed my writing and made my intellectual and spiritual understanding of a traveling life more abundant.

Larry Butler has been my friend, cheerleader and fellow so-journer whose commitment and activism continually calls us to consider what's right and true. With others who care, Larry engages in respectful debate about the political, economic, social, and natural forces that cross one another to affect the global community. As it pertains to this book, I'm grateful to Larry and his discussion group who wrestle with the pressing questions that affect the mobile community.

Sandra Haven has my deep gratitude for providing tactful and forthright direction to this book. Working with Sandra is like taking a master class in writing and no writer could ask for a better editor. Thanks also to my dear friends Karen Anderson, Pat Sylvanen and Missy Henderson for taking a first look and giving great feedback. We may be scattered far and wide, but our friendships span time and distance easily.

Thank you also to my Rooted Community of friends and family who waved reluctant good-byes as Arnie and I bid farewell and drove off into the sunset for parts unknown. I know what you were thinking and thank you for always being supportive anyway.

I owe a debt of gratitude to all of the my fellow wanderers who participated in the interviews for this work. Thank you so much for trusting me and sharing your stories with me.

I also wish to remember Ed Cox, who has wandered from this world now and whose soul now swims with the whales off the coast of California. Ed was a philosopher, and a gentleman whose life's passion was creating an inclusive place to live for all people no matter what their means. Sadly, he never truly found his own place, but he did inspire others to think about, write about and practice what it means to be a part of a community. For that, I remember him with love.

My husband Arnie has shared every mile of the adventure with me and run necessary daily interference so that this book could take form. When two old friends find each other a second time, karmic magic happens. I love you truly.

And finally, I want to acknowledge my love and respect for Scott Buckland, my adventurous wandering child, alternative thinker and natural master of community-making. You always draw a warm circle of friendship wherever you go, and your many friends love you across the distance and years.

About the Author
Barbara Wentzell Jaquith

Barbara Jaquith is an artist, writer and community activist who loves helping others realize their dreams. In between wanderings, she is currently building community in Conyers, Georgia with her husband, two dogs Wicca and Journey, and an African Grey parrot named Cracker.

Made in the USA
Middletown, DE
16 February 2022

61314586R00116